ONE HUNDRED YEARS OF HARTT

———————

Michelle Anne Robert,

Thank you for your

wonderful help—

Best Wishes,

Dee

HartfordBooks

HartfordBooks is a book series developed in partnership with the University of Hartford that seeks to rediscover the Capital City by publishing books about Hartford's vibrant and influential people, history, and culture. The series is supported by the University of Hartford and the Hartford Foundation for Public Giving.

ONE HUNDRED YEARS OF HARTT

A Centennial Celebration of The Hartt School

DEMARIS HANSEN

Foreword by Steve Metcalf

Wesleyan University Press
Middletown, Connecticut

Wesleyan University Press
Middletown CT 06459
www.wesleyan.edu/wepress
© 2020 Demaris Hansen

Designed by Rachel Rosa
Production by John Nordyke
Typeset in Stoneprint and Essonnes

This book is part of HartfordBooks,
a series developed through a partnership
with Wesleyan University Press and
the University of Hartford,
and supported by
the Hartford Foundation for Public Giving.

//wesleyan.edu/wespress/hartfordbooks

Printed in China
Library of Congress Cataloging-in-Publication Data
available upon request

5 4 3 2 1

Hardcover ISBN: 978-0-8195-7952-2
Ebook ISBN: 978-0-8195-7953-9

CONTENTS

vi   HARTT LEADERSHIP

vii   FOREWORD BY STEVE METCALF

xiii   AUTHOR'S NOTE

1   CHAPTER 1   *The Early Years*

27   CHAPTER 2   *Formation of the University of Hartford*

41   CHAPTER 3   *The Hartt School Community Division*

57   CHAPTER 4   *Programs, Degrees, and Services*

99   CHAPTER 5   *A New Century: A Performing Arts Institution (1990–2020)*

111   INTO THE FUTURE

112   ACKNOWLEDGMENTS

114   APPENDIX

116   REFERENCES AND INDEX

HARTT LEADERSHIP

Julius Hartt	1920 – 1934
Moshe Paranov	1934 – 1971
Donald Mattran	1971 – 1980
Donald Harris	1980 – 1988

Interim Deans
    Manuel Alvarez
    Stuart Schar
	1988 – 1990

Larry Alan Smith	1990 – 1997
Malcolm Morrison	1998 – 2008
Aaron Flagg	2009 – 2014
Interim Dean Clark Saunders	2014 – 2016
Betsy Cooper	2016 – 2018
Larry Alan Smith	2018 – PRESENT

FOREWORD *Steve Metcalf*

In the fall of 1964, as I was beginning my senior year of high school in Schenectady, New York my longtime piano teacher asked me what colleges I was going to apply to. I said I didn't know. I knew I wanted to pursue music somehow or other, but otherwise I didn't have much of a game plan. She said there was a school in Connecticut that I should look into. On its faculty was a pianist she knew of, and she thought he might be a good person for me to study with.

The school was the Hartt College of Music, in Hartford, Connecticut. I had never heard of the school, but on my teacher's advice I applied. A few months later I drove over to Hartford to visit, and to audition. Hartt was part of the recently founded University of Hartford, whose grassy suburban campus had just opened a year and a half earlier. Truth to tell, in those days it wasn't much of a campus — just a handful of buildings and a lot of lawn. But the buildings were handsome and new, and the place had an open, promising kind of feel. I had taken a couple of auditions already, and I was prepared for what I had come to assume was the standard tenor of these things: *All right, tell us what you have prepared.* Followed by, *Thank you, we'll let you know.* By contrast, the people at Hartt who greeted and interviewed me were friendly, engaging. The man who listened to my audition somehow wound up talking to me about baseball and politics, along with Beethoven and Poulenc. It turned out that the person my piano teacher had mentioned was no longer on the Hartt faculty. But the school, and its welcoming vibe, had made an impression on me.

A couple of months later, when it came time to decide where I would go, I chose Hartt. As I soon discovered, it was a place with a seemingly endless cast of vivid personalities.

Among them:

– The cosmopolitan, Ferrari-driving composer Arnold Franchetti (1906–1993), whose father had been a friend of Puccini, and who told us stories about having escaped—on foot, through the Alps—the Fascist regime in Italy, and of having turned up later in Munich, where he took lessons with Richard Strauss;

– The stylish, pixie-like pianist and vocal coach Irene Kahn (1904–1996), who would joke about her vast collection of shoes one moment, and then, without missing a beat—literally—sit down at the piano and cold sight-read a thorny twentieth-century opera score as if she had known it for years;

– Joseph Iadone (1914–2004), one of the great lute players of the 20th century and a brilliant teacher of ear training and sight-singing, who nevertheless, with his shambling gait and impish mustache, looked as if he might have been a character created by Peter Sellers;

– Edward Miller (1930–2013), a wry and cerebral composer by day and hard-swinging jazz player (valve trombone, mostly) by night. Professor Miller's local standing rocketed upward, at least among some of us, when we learned that he was a good friend of legendary *Mad* magazine cartoonist Don Martin;

– In a different category, I can recall occasionally glimpsing the courtly Alfred "A.C." Fuller (1885–1973), who was known around the world for having created the Fuller Brush Company. Starting in the 1930s, Fuller had become the school's principal donor and benefactor, and Hartt old timers always went out of their way to acknowledge that the school would have never succeeded without him.

But the dominant personality of this personality-rich school was its co-founder and, for more than half a century its unquestioned leader, Moshe Paranov (1895–1994). In the pages of this remarkable book by Dee Hansen, you will come to know "Uncle" Moshe, as he invited the students to call him, more fully. But even to a clueless 17-year-old college freshman, it was apparent that this was an exceptional human being. His welcoming talk to the incoming students was short on conventional pleasantries. Instead, he dispensed a rapid-fire assortment of his signature homespun quips and cautions:

*So your aunt Matilda thinks you're a musical genius. That's wonderful, but I've got news for you —
the rest of the world couldn't care less.*

*You call yourself a musician because you know Beethoven's Fifth? Well, what about Monteverdi's
Orfeo? Or the piano concerto of Busoni? Or the songs of Wolf? And when you learn those, come and
see me. I'll give you a few hundred more.*

*Music is a great gift, but it's a tough way to make a living. That's because the average person today
doesn't know Beethoven from a ham sandwich.*

There's no such thing as too much practicing. Keep going—it can always be better.

The origins of The Hartt School, as it was eventually renamed, could hardly have been more
improbable. Briefly, in the fall of 1920, Paranov, then a twenty-five year-old aspiring pianist,
joined with his mentor and future father-in-law, one Julius Hartt (who made his living, such
as it was, as a newspaper music critic), Hartt's pianist daughter Pauline—soon to be Moshe's
wife—and one or two colleagues, to hang their collective shingle outside Julius's residence
on a leafy street in Hartford. They paid themselves pittances when they could afford to pay
themselves at all. (The tradition of faculty salaries that were, to use Paranov's own word,
"laughable," was to continue for many years.)

Yet by and by the school managed to grow to the point where it was able to move, first to a
larger house, and then, in 1938, to a handsome, turreted brick edifice that had previously
been home to the Hartford Seminary. Paranov assembled a first-rate faculty and expanded
the school's curriculum to include music education, composition, conducting, and all the
other disciplines required for a proper, accredited conservatory. He also brought to Hartford
an astonishing procession of visiting eminences, including pianists Harold Bauer and Dame
Myra Hess, violinist Isaac Stern, soprano Eileen Farrell, composers William Schuman and
Aaron Copland, and scores of others.

How did he do this, exactly?

Sheer pluck seems to have played a major role. Moshe himself once told me years ago about
a phone call he made to the celebrated cellist Leonard Rose, asking if he would come up from
New York to give a couple of master classes. Hearing the puny honorarium, Rose begged

off. Moshe persisted, sweetening the offer with the promise of a home-cooked Jewish dinner featuring his specialty, sautéed whitefish. Sensing that Rose might be wavering, Moshe went on to describe in detail the homemade cornmeal-based batter that he used, right down to the seasonings. Rose said he would be up before the end of the week.

*

A hundred years is a long time, especially in musical terms. It's the amount of time between the premiere of Beethoven's Ninth and the premiere of *Rhapsody in Blue.* There must have been moments when Moshe and his troupe wondered if their school would make it through the next semester, much less survive for a century. We know the school's finances were particularly shaky during the Depression and World War II. (According to lore, in some of those lean times the aforementioned Mr. Fuller would be called upon to personally cover the school's end-of-year deficit. The lore says that he did so, repeatedly.)

The decision to become part of the new University of Hartford, in 1957, was pivotal, of course—the end of one era and beginning of another. If the change meant a certain loss of independence, it also meant stability and fresh opportunities for growth. Moshe officially retired in 1971, but the school marched on. It added a jazz major, overseen by the alto sax virtuoso Jackie McLean. Its opera program acquired a national reputation. It continued to host a string of "name" visitors: Marian Anderson, Mstislav Rostropovich, Yehudi Menuhin, Dizzy Gillespie, Karl Bohm, John Cage, Wynton Marsalis. In the early eighties it signed a young, unheralded string quartet to an informal residency. The group called itself the Emerson Quartet, in honor of Ralph Waldo. The residency wound up lasting twenty-one years, during which time the group gradually took its place as the perhaps the preeminent string quartet of our time.

Crucially, the school officially added degree programs in dance and theatre in the mid-nineties. In a kind of small sub-miracle of its own, those new disciplines quickly flourished and became as much a part of the fabric of the school as music.

And now, almost suddenly in some ways, Hartt finds itself on the eve of its centennial. These days, when I'm at the school for a meeting or event, I make a point of taking note of the sights and sounds coming from the rows of practice rooms and rehearsal spaces. I find it's as good a way as any to savor the breadth and range of the place.

In recent days, walking the corridors—sometimes at the Fuller building where the music activities are housed, and sometimes at the newer Handel Center, which is home to the dance and theatre programs—I have randomly overheard:

A pianist struggling (heroically) to smooth out a passage in Chopin's *Heroic Polonaise*; a young woman in the music theatre program singing "Promises, Promises" (I couldn't help wondering if she knew that the artist who made that song famous—the great Dionne Warwick—is a Hartt alum); the orchestra rehearsing the deceptively modern Fifth Symphony of Sibelius; the jazz ensemble wailing on an updated arrangement of Stevie Wonder's *Sir Duke*; the wind ensemble playing the heck out of Samuel Barber's *Commando March*; a dance class warming up to an old Gladys Knight and the Pips song; a trumpet player rehearsing that instrument's famous solo in Stravinsky's *Petrushka*; a violinist boldly taking on the daredevil final section of Max Bruch's *Scottish Fantasy*.

At these moments, I often think of Uncle Moshe. I can't be sure what he would have made of his school having reached the century mark. Some mixture of pride and amazement, I'm guessing.

What I *can* say is that he would have undoubtedly stuck his head into some of these practice rooms, or, come to think of it maybe each and every one of them, and said, "Good, that's good. Now keep going—it can always be better."

STEVE METCALF (HARTT, B.M., 1970)
May 2019

AUTHOR'S NOTE

For over one hundred years the communities surrounding Hartford, Connecticut, have been enriched by the extraordinary talents of students, faculty, and guest artists from The Hartt School. From its meager beginnings, the school thrived on the determination and deeply held beliefs of its founders. Their love of music and teaching was the compass that provided direction for the school's stellar reputation through time. The story of The Hartt School is best told through volumes of letters, newspaper articles, oral histories, and its performances and productions. It is a joyful history, full of colorful personas who were beset by the challenges of wars and financial burdens. Yet, despite many potentially destructive barriers, the school persevered and today continues to serve as a beacon of artistic excellence in the Hartford community and across the nation.

The aim of this book and the accompanying centennial website is to bring to life those people and events that made *One Hundred Years of Hartt* possible. In doing so, the deep and enduring connections between The Hartt School and the Hartford community will enlighten us about the vibrant cultural life of Hartford, both past and present. The partnerships are rich and deep, including the Asylum Hill Congregational Church, the *Hartford Times* and *Hartford Courant* newspapers, Kingswood-Oxford School, the WTIC radio station, the Horace Bushnell Memorial Hall, the Hartford Symphony Orchestra, St. Joseph's College, Hartford Theological Seminary, the Hartford Musical Foundation, the Hartford Jewish community and Beth Israel Temple, the Cathedral of St. Joseph, the Hartford Ballet, the Connecticut Commission on the Arts, local school districts and churches, and the Mark Twain family. Strong, decades-old ties to Hartford dance and theatre companies led to the creation of degrees and expansion of the collegiate and community divisions in the 1990s.

In 1957 the Hartt College of Music, Hillyer College, and the Hartford Art School were consolidated to form the University of Hartford. Alfred C. Fuller, a Hartford resident and businessman, whose generous donations resulted in the Alfred C. Fuller Music Center on the University of Hartford campus, made the future home of our school possible. Scores of notable Hartford families and businesses were integral to the history of the school as well. The book consists of five parts: The Early Years; Formation of the University of Hartford; The Julius Hartt School of Music/Community Division Programs, Degrees, and Services; and A New Century: A Performing Arts Institution (1990–2020). Undoubtedly, there will be names and stories not mentioned in this overview of Hartt's history. But it is my hope that scholars and historians will be motivated to further investigate the inspiring people, events, and institutions involved with our remarkable school.

―――――――――

ONE HUNDRED YEARS OF HARTT

The Julius Hartt School of Music.

An institution devoted to comprehensive musical education.

188 Sigourney Street

Hartford, Connecticut.

A sketch of the Julius Hartt School of Music, first located at 188 Sigourney Street in Hartford.

1 | THE EARLY YEARS

❝ *Education is a continuous process. Culture is a progressive study. It admits of no standstill. It is a habit of mind, not an inert accumulation of knowledge. And when it ceases to progress it really ceases to exist. No one can study music to much purpose if he shuts himself up to the study of music exclusively. It is at this point that so many would-be-musicians fall down.*

Julius Hartt, *Letters of a Musician,*
"Letter to a Young Lady," 1918

THE FOUNDERS AND THEIR FAMILIES

In 1920 Julius Hartt, his daughter Pauline Hartt, Morris Perlmutter, and Samuel Berkman founded the Julius Hartt School of Music and began operations from the Hartt home at 188 Sigourney in Hartford, Connecticut. They soon moved to 222 Collins Street. Pauline, though only twenty-one at the time, had already proven herself to be a strong, savvy businesswoman. Morris Perlmutter, who later changed his name to Moshe Paranov, and

Samuel Berkman were students of Julius Hartt. Together with Julius Hartt they devoted their energy and passion for music and provided the pillars of strength needed to found and build a school. They shared in the purchase of the school's first house on Collins Street, as well as pianos and other equipment. In the beginning the four founders were $20,000 in debt. Over the years, they began paying off the debt, but financial challenges persisted throughout time. Their belief in the value of musical training was critical in growing and sustaining the school. The founders each had unique and interesting stories prior to and during the early years of the school.

JULIUS HARTT (1869–1942)

Though The Hartt School is named after Julius Hartt, today not much is known about him. Julius Hartt did not leave an autobiography informing us of his years of study or of his attempts to found and guide a school through its early years. He did, however, leave a wealth of written materials, including letters and newspaper articles, that provide a lens into his astute mind and passion for music.

Julius Hartt was born in 1869 in Boston, the son of Reverend Aaron Hartt, a Baptist minister, and Helen Marr Hartt. Hartt studied piano with Louis Maas and Carl Baermann, both well known as outstanding pupils of Liszt. He married Jennie Hall and fathered three children before traveling to Europe in 1902 to study with Ernest Jedlizka, a pupil of Arthur Rubenstein. He became a personal friend of the legendary pianist Theordor Leschetizky. He studied composition with Wilhelm Berger, who was a famous composer and teacher at the Klindwerth-Schwarwenka conservatory and a pupil of Brahms.

Berger advised Hartt that beautiful playing only happens when one's technique is so fluent that one's playing reflects one's own soul or nature. Julius Hartt brought this philosophy of artistic musicianship with him when he returned to Boston with his family in 1903. There he wrote *Casual Affirmations of a Pianist* (date unknown), which appears to be a pamphlet that articulates Hartt's philosophy as a teacher of the pianoforte and also offers times when he is available to give lessons.

Hartt wrote a series of six articles called *Letters of a Musician,* written between 1917 and 1918 when he was the music editor of the *Hartford Times*. Throughout his *Letters of a Musician,* Hartt's vision for education was profound and timeless. The letters spoke of the significance of music and art as part of the

Young Julius Hartt sitting at a piano

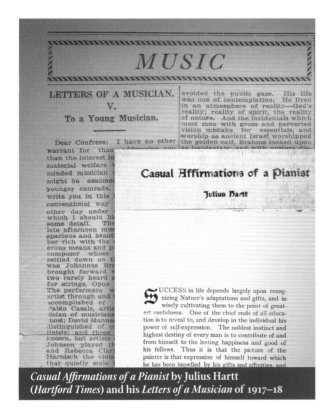

Casual Affirmations of a Pianist by Julius Hartt (*Hartford Times*) and his *Letters of a Musician* of 1917–18

Julius Hartt's beliefs provided the foundational philosophy of the school that today, one hundred years later, still bears his name.

The letters were full of insightful perspectives, and many remain relevant today. Dr. Myron Schwager, associate professor of music history at the University of Hartford for 19 years, quoted Ernest Bloch in an 1985 *American Music* article. Bloch, the renowned composer and artist-in-residence, wrote about Julius Hartt's philosophy and contributions as reflected in Hartt's *Letters of a Musician,*

> " *Hartt was a music educator of uncommon vision and accomplishments as indicated in the words of praise lavished upon him by reputed musicians and scholars. [His] words sometimes tend to be flowery and perhaps even exaggerated; but if they bear the stamp of a bygone era, their message is clear: Julius Hartt was considered an important, even prophetic figure for the future of music in America.*

Julius married Jennie (whom he also called Jane) in 1898. His letters revealed a deeply devoted and loving relationship with his wife and children. Julius referred to himself as "Pa" to the children and sometimes called himself "Bob" when writing to Jane. The letters to and from Jane (Jennie) and his children, Pauline (Dot), Harriet (Gizzy), and Robert, were donated to the University of Hartford archives by Pauline Hartt Paranov. When Julius was abroad, he wrote often

development of a well-rounded person. In them he also relayed a philosophy gleaned from his teacher Berger. He wrote in "Letter to a Young Man," February 9, 1918,

> " *Please believe me that the only real technique in the world is the power to express something that you feel…. An ounce of musical and artistic inspiration will advance you further on your way than a ton of technical pedagogy…. I counsel you to sing…. If you cannot sing try to sing.*

about how much he missed Jane and "the babies." In 1902 he wrote a compelling letter that asks the family to come live with him in Berlin. His letter is notable for its rationale for them to join him, and in particular his desire for Jane to have an equal opportunity for personal growth.

THE LETTER TO JANE

December 14, 1902
Berlin, Germany

Dear Jane,

From my point of view I am convinced that it is our only wise course for you and the family to come over here as soon as spring opens up and arrangements can be made there. I will tell you why. In the first place I am feeling more and more day by day that if we are to take the place in life which we wish, it is as important that you have privileges as it is that I do—perhaps more so. You could make yourself just as susceptible to development as I am and there is a certain very tangible something which comes to women as to men from contact with foreign lips. Of itself it always gives ours a distinguishing quality which is valuable and a potent means toward the accomplishment of ends such as we have envisioned.... and a married man cannot go into society without his wife—at least we wouldn't. And if you and I are going to do this sort of thing, as we must, then for your own self-confidence and for the help you can be to me by working this end of the business, it is very important that you have these opportunities for musical culture and for gaining prestige which comes from life over here.

From another standpoint it is wrong in principle for the husband to have everything in the way of privileges and fine friends and the wife nothing; and there is no reason why such a family should be a happy one; and every reason to expect that the children in it are going to suffer...as a consequence... I am by nature too unselfish to my having things which I cannot share with those whom I love... And I do love my wife as I never loved anyone unless it is my babies and I can't bear to go on in this selfish way for two years.

As ever, Bob [Julius]

Many Hartt family letters are preserved in the University of Hartford Archives. They reveal a sense of humor, a tight family bond, and how the challenges of war and economic depression affected their lives. Julius Hartt's values and beliefs provided the energy and foundation for the school of music which bears his name. His beloved Jennie died in 1932, prior to the formation of the Julius Hartt Musical Foundation (JHMF). Julius suffered a long illness and died on September 9, 1942. He reluctantly submitted his letter of resignation from the Hartford Musical Foundation in 1935 when he was no longer able to contribute to the foundation and school.

MOSHE PARANOV (1895–1994) EARLY LIFE EXPERIENCES

Morris Perlmutter (Moshe Paranov) was one of Julius Hartt's first pupils. He became the best known cofounder of The Hartt School. Through the 98 years of his life, Moshe Paranov was an integral part of the Hartford community.

Perlmutter served in World War I as a sergeant in the 12th Division, 73rd Infantry Band. He was promoted to the rank of band sergeant while stationed with the U.S. Army at Fort Devens, Massachusetts, September 24, 1918.

SPECIAL MEETING OF THE CORPORATION

HARTFORD MUSICAL FOUNDATION, INC.

A special meeting of the members of the Hartford Musical Foundation, Inc., was held in the offices of the Corporation in Hartford on Thursday, September 12, at 4:15 o'clock P.M.. *1935*

VOTED: To accept with regret the resignation of Julius Hartt as a member of the Corporation effective as of this date.

VOTED: To elect as a member of the Corporation Pauline Hartt Paranov to fill the vacancy created by the resignation of Mr. Hartt.

The meeting then adjourned.

Respectfully submitted,

Temporary Clerk

The special notice to the Julius Hartt Board of Trustees (September 12, 1935)

Moshe Paranov at the piano with his teacher Julius Hartt, circa 1918.

The promotion came as a bit of surprise due to his lack of knowledge about music history that was uncovered in his interview for the position. On December 18, 1918, Morris wrote a letter to the commander of the 73rd Infantry Division requesting that he be discharged so that he could return to a small music school in Connecticut that needed him. Around this time he changed his birth name from Morris Perlmutter to Moshe Paranov as he began his professional career as a pianist.

Many of Moshe's letters to Pauline (or Dot) while he was in the army were written partially or completely in French. In the letter [opposite], he proclaims that he is not worthy of her, and not nearly as handsome as

David, presumably an unidentified suitor of Dottie's. In her letters, Jennie Hartt, Dot's mother, was not at all certain about her daughter's relationship with an older man.

Morris Permutter (Moshe Paranov) and Pauline Hartt met when she was 12 years old and he was 16. Moshe became her piano teacher at that time. He said, "*At that time I was only in love with my music but we were together day in and day out. And I fell in love with her and she fell in love with me. I was pursuing my career like mad and she was pursuing her career like mad and we decided to pursue them together.*" In 1924 they married. Their union lasted for 52 years until her death.

In 1921, Moshe first performed at the Aeolian Hall in New York City, and in 1922 he played at Boston's Jordan Hall. Moshe would go on to perform concertos with the New York Philharmonic and collaborate with leading musicians in the world such as Mstislav Rostropovich and Dimitri Shostakovich; he even directed the world premiere of William Schuman's opera *The Mighty Casey*. Julius Hartt had earlier introduced Moshe to Ernest Bloch, the noted Swiss composer, who recognized his talents,

> 66 *My friend Hartt has a young pupil of 21 years who is absolutely extraordinary as a musician and pianist. This boy's name is Morris Perlmutter, and I am convinced he is a real genius.... This boy, who in 3 days learns by heart a whole Brahms sonata, is a modest and simple boy — humble and without a shadow of pretention. He does not enthuse, and does not live except under the inspiration of music.*

In 1926 Paranov joined the music staff at WTIC radio and became the music director in 1938. He was conductor of the Hartford Hospital Training School Glee Club and the Cecelia Club of Hartford. On January 14, 1930, Paranov continued his significant outreach into the Hartford community by conducting the Choral Club of Hartford, the Hartford Oratorio Society, and the Cecelia Club, accompanied by fifty musicians from the Boston Symphony Orchestra for the opening dedication of the Horace Bushnell

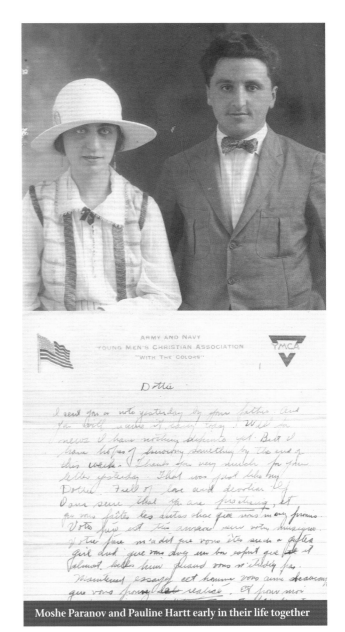

Moshe Paranov and Pauline Hartt early in their life together

Memorial Hall. Paranov continued a close relationship with the Bushnell and in 1934 performed Bach's *Concerto in C* for three pianos with Harold Bauer and Ossip Gabrilowitsch, son-in-law of Mark Twain, at the Bushnell Memorial Hall. During the first eight years of its existence every public concert of the music school was presented there, either in the Colonial Room or in the large hall.

By 1941 the world war forced cancellation of the Hartford Symphony Orchestra concert season due to of lack of musicians and funding. In 1946 the local

THE HORACE BUSHNELL MEMORIAL HALL

Presents

Harold Bauer *and*
Ossip Gabrilowitsch
in a two-piano recital

ASSISTED BY

MOSHE PARANOV

Wednesday Evening, January 24, 1934
at 8:15 o'clock

Moshe Paranov performed at Horace Bushnell Memorial Hall with Mark Twain's son-in-law and Harold Bauer.

musicians' union agreed to perform four concerts for free to help revive the symphony. Through the generosity of Francis Goodwin, considered by some "the father of the Hartford Symphony," Willard B. Rogers, president of the HSO board, the Travelers Insurance Company, and radio station WTIC-FM, restructuring and new financing enabled the symphony to officially restart. Moshe Paranov and former concertmaster and assistant conductor of the orchestra George Heck led the concerts of the 1948–1949 season, with Paranov conducting the first concert. Fund-raising and enthusiasm returned to the Hartford Symphony as a result of the collaborative efforts of the community.

Paranov's lengthy service to the Hartford community included serving on the Connecticut Commission on the Arts beginning in 1963. He first began teaching music at the Kingswood School when it was located in the Mark Twain House in the late 1920s, and, was affiliated with the school for over 70 years. He was an artist-in-residence in the Watkinson School, as well as the Farmington, Torrington, Glastonbury, and Simsbury schools. Paranov directed the Hartford Hospital chorus for seventeen years and frequently conducted the Hartford Symphony Orchestra. Over time, he was fondly referred to as "Uncle Moshe."

Through his lifetime, Moshe Paranov was duly recognized for his work. He received an honorary doctor of dine arts degree from Hillyer College and was appointed vice-chancellor for Performing Arts in 1957. He received the University of Hartford University Medal for Distinguished Public Service in 1969. In 1971 he became president emeritus of the Hartt College of Music. He was awarded the A. C. Fuller Medal in 1984.

Moshe Paranov's inspirational beliefs and indefatigable drive are fondly remembered by those alums, faculty, and staff who knew him. His director's reports to the JHMF Board of Trustees reveal a man dedicated to furthering beauty in life through music and art. Moshe's dedication to beauty in all its forms was manifested in his love of photography. He wrote,

> *Too many camera buffs think the only requirement for taking good pictures is thousands of dollars' worth of expensive equipment. They run around clicking what they think is a picture and, alas, the end result is complete failure. The camera cannot do it alone. One must see, feel and create the picture or the finished product is a print which says nothing.*
>
> *I can honestly say that I get the same thrill out of a good performance as I do when I have created a good picture. Infinite patience, a great deal of hard work and endless study are needed to compose a piece of music or to take a good picture. It takes a lifetime to understand either. That's what makes creativity such an exciting adventure.*

Monhegan. *Photograph by Moshe Paranov*

Moshe Paranov's pipes

9

PAULINE HARTT (1899–1981)

Pauline (Dottie) Hartt was born on September 3, 1899, the oldest child of Jane and Julius Hartt. She was named after her mother's foster mother, Pauline Lilly, though called Dot or Dottie by her family and friends. Her earliest memories are of living in Berlin for nearly two years where her father, Julius, studied to be a concert pianist. In her memoirs she confirms that her father returned to America to bring her mother, sister, and foster mother, Pauline Lilly (Dot's namesake) to Germany because he greatly missed them.

Pauline (Dot) Hartt and her piano teacher, Harold Bauer.

In the beginning days of the Julius Hartt School of Music during World War I, the teachers, who were mostly men, were called to service. Pauline recalled that her father did not want her to teach, but no one was left but the two of them, so as an accomplished pianist, she began teaching piano in 1917. She also received instruction in harmony and composition from composer Ernest Bloch. During her lifetime she studied music with her father and Moshe Paranov, Harold Bauer, Rubin Goldmark, and Alfred Einstein.

As an original founder of The Hartt School, Pauline worked tirelessly to establish a strong and viable school of music. During Pauline's 60 years of service, for which she received a Medal for Distinguished Service Citation in 1979, Pauline served as Hartt dean of students, 1936–1949, and as associate dean of students, University of Hartford, 1962–1974. She was the chairman of the Department of Music History at Hartt from 1949–1957, as well as the chair of the Department of Piano Pedagogy from 1949–1958. Clearly, her contributions to the school were incalculable. She also served as head of the music departments at the Fernwood and Kingswood Schools in Hartford. Her work with Elemer Nagy as costumer for the Hartt Opera-Theater overlapped her other responsibilities from 1942 until 1969. In a May 2, 1955, article in the *Hartford Times*, Nagy commented,

Pauline Hartt (L) working in the Hartt costume shop

> **"** *Mrs. Paranov has a keen sense of exactly duplicating the sketches I give her. She cuts her own patterns, not even using standard sleeve or bodice outlines, and cuts them to the measurements of the people singing the roles for which the costumes are intended. She confesses to some difficulty in getting the accurate measurements of the girls' waistlines. They have a habit of writing down what they wish they had in inches rather than the actual ones!*

The adopted daughters of Moshe and Dot followed in their parent's footsteps as contributors to the school's work.

Tanya (1933–2006) was well recognized as the director of the Children's Musical Theater as well as the director of the Children's Singing School. Nina Paranov Fagan today is honored for her work to preserve audio recordings of students, faculty, and guest artists for decades at The Hartt School. Her presence continues to be a remarkable testament to the persistence and values of the school's founding principles.

Tanya and Nina Paranov as children

A young Sam Berkman

SAMUEL BERKMAN (1893–1987)

Samuel Berkman was born in Hartford, Connecticut, in 1893. He graduated from Hartford High School in 1912 and from Trinity College with a bachelor of arts degree in 1916. Berkman began study of the piano at the age of twelve. He studied piano with Julius Hartt beginning in 1911 and throughout his studies at Trinity College. In 1916 he joined Julius Hartt and Morris Perlmutter (Moshe Paranov) upon his graduation from Trinity to form an association called the "Julius Hartt, Moshe Paranov and Associated Teachers." After brief service in the navy from 1918 to 1919, Sam returned to Hartford to devote his energy chiefly to the interests of the association, officially established as a music school in Julius Hartt's home at 188 Sigourney Street in Hartford. He performed many concerts in the Hartford area, including the first concert of the Cecelia Club.

Sam Berkman was an important, visionary leader in the efforts to institute curriculum planning for high school music in the Hartford area and the state of Connecticut. He chaired Region 6 of the National Association of Schools of Music (NASM). His leadership in NASM helped establish critical accreditation standards and practices for postsecondary universities and colleges. He was the motivating force that led to the Julius Hartt School of Music's first accreditation with the National Association of Schools of Music in 1947. He was an active member of the Trinity Club, the Kiwanis Club, the Wadsworth Atheneum, and the Symphony Society of Greater Hartford. He also taught at St. Joseph College and the Kingswood School.

In his report from the 1964 Connecticut Advisory Committee on Music Education, he relayed the beliefs of the committee regarding foundational courses needed to prepare students for music study in college, including knowledge of notation, pitch, rhythms, keys, key signatures, scales, musical terms, solfège or sight singing and ear training, basic harmonic concepts, major styles and masterpieces of musical literature, and piano proficiency. In 1964 Berkman was awarded an honorary degree of doctor of music by the University of Hartford.

Samuel Berkman teaching at the Julius Hartt School of Music at 187 Broad Street

IRENE KAHN

Irene Kahn was born Irene Cohen, the daughter of Latvian immigrants. She used the name Irene Kahn as an adult and after her marriage to Samuel Berkman in 1925.

Samuel Berkman and his wife Irene Kahn Berkman

Berkman worked with many Hartford and state councils to propose standards for state approval of teacher education standards in music education training and to create a statement of duties for a state fine arts consultant.

Sam was known for his outstanding wit, a far-ranging mind, impeccable musicianship, aesthetic awareness, linguistic proficiency, and penetrating scholarship. His legacy continues today through The Hartt School performances and programs that regularly occur in Berkman Auditorium within the Fuller Building.

Their son, John, was a double major in violin and piano at the Julius Hartt School of Music. He became a recognized musician and recipient of the Hartt Alumnus of the Year Award in 1986.

Irene Kahn Berkman and son John practicing his violin

13

Irene, who joined the Hartt faculty in 1924, was an instructor of piano, theory, and opera. She also taught at St. Joseph's College and the University of Connecticut. She was remembered as the driving force behind many Hartt concerts and productions. She authored a textbook on piano technique, composed, coached, accompanied, and served as a production manager for Hartt Opera-Theater. Irene performed many legendary duo piano concerts with Moshe Paranov.

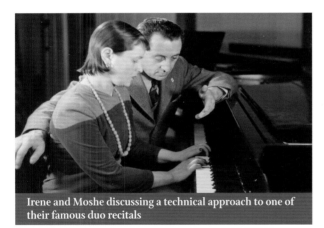

Irene and Moshe discussing a technical approach to one of their famous duo recitals

Irene was highly regarded for her extraordinary musicality as well as her authentic Chinese gowns and black horn-rimmed glasses. Irene's grandson Daniel accepted the Hartt Hall of Fame award on her behalf in 2017 and donated two of Irene's dresses to the Connecticut Historical Society in Hartford. Irene passed away on April 20, 1996, shortly after celebrating her 92nd birthday.

A SCHOOL IS BORN
THE FOUNDING OF THE JULIUS HARTT SCHOOL OF MUSIC (1920–1921)

> *The Julius Hartt School of Music believes in the mission of music in everyday life, but it does not believe that music is an independent entity. Its belief, on the contrary, is that music is but one aspect of an all comprehensive whole, and that that whole may be called education; that it is in reality life; that life is art; and that art is nature moulded in the crucible of law, of discipline, and of experience.*
>
> The First Catalogue

The Julius Hartt School of Music
1920=1921

The cover and dates of the Julius Hartt School of Music in its First Catalogue

The music school, first located in Hartt's home at 188 Sigourney Street in Hartford, began with a faculty of men and women who quickly established themselves as proficient and respected educators. The group bought and moved to a home at 222 Collins Street in 1920. The four founders were joined in the early years by outstanding musicians including Ernst Bloch, Irene Kahn, Harold Bauer, Eva Gautier, Margaret Warner, and others, all of whom were the cornerstone of the school.

In the early years the school had very little money with which to entice outstanding visiting faculty. Somehow, and most likely due to the persuasion of the founders and the kindness they imparted to their many artist friends, the school attracted highly recognized and celebrated performers to teach master classes and support their cause.

When the school opened in 1920, the founders, Julius Hartt, Morris Perlmutter (Moshe Paranov), Pauline Hartt, and Samuel Berkman, presented a catalogue of information that described the instructors, courses, beliefs and values, and additional information about the school. The First Catalogue 1920–1921 conveyed many of Julius Hartt's sentiments from his *Letters to a Musician*, influenced by his teachers in Europe in the early 1900s.

The belief in a comprehensive education is reflected in the courses offered from the initial academic year of the school. In 1927 a college department was inaugurated and the first college courses were offered.

Teachers and Teaching To teach and to be taught, to be taught through teaching; to give and to receive, to receive in giving; the teacher to learn of the pupil, the pupil to learn of the teacher; reciprocal education: this is the fundamental philosophy upon which the Julius Hartt School of Music bases its practice and its hope of usefulness. This school begins its institutional caree   and persis   the belief   are obsol   orm-ance   pose entire   lines of tra   must be ta   t by pupils   to a level   cher at all   e of susce   s his pupil   the highe

believ   astly like   raph-cient   effi-or of   aster can   n he that   omb; be a   can to co   eking super   hable own   iality visual   being larger   at he cann   enus old-fashioned but happily becoming extinct — a species of teacher that has been all too common in

THE JULIUS HARTT SCHOOL OF MUSIC

Julius Hartt, Boris Paranov, Directors

Ernest Bloch, Artistic Advisor

Faculty

Nathan H. Allen, Organ, Composition, Theoretical Subjects

Samuel Berkman, A.B., Pianoforte, Academic Subjects

Ernest Bloch, Affiliated Teacher. Higher Composition

(Mrs.) Genevieve Allen Case, Pianoforte, History of Music

Charles Cheney, Science of Pianoforte Tuning, Voicing, Regulating and Repairing

(Mme.) Adrienne Remenyi Von Ende and Assistants, Singing.

(Mrs.) Jennie A. Hartt, Musical Kindergarten and Pianoforte Fundamentals

(Miss) Pauline Hartt, Pianoforte

Julius Hartt, Pianoforte, Higher Composition, Ensemble

(Mlle.) Marguerite Koch, French

Franz Milcke, and Assistants, Violin and Ensemble

Boris Paranov (Morris Perlmutter), Pianoforte, Harmony, Counterpoint

(Miss) Elsie Teal, Pianoforte

(Miss) Margaret Warner, B.A., M.A., Modern Languages

Experienced artist teachers and Assistants, Ensemble and Orchestral Instruments

The first faculty of the Julius Hartt School of Music, 1920–1921.

Harold Bauer, Irene Kahn, and Moshe Paranov in concert, Rubin Segal conducting.

EARLY GUEST ARTISTS AND FACULTY

HAROLD BAUER

As a famed pianist, Harold Bauer's relationship with Julius Hartt, Moshe Paranov, and the Hartt School was significant, given the exceptional breadth of his professional contacts and performance career. Julius Hartt met Harold Bauer in 1902 while Hartt was in London. By 1932 Harold Bauer had become a valued guest artist and visiting teacher at the Hartt School. Concerts featuring Harold and the Hartt faculty were enthusiastically acclaimed.

In his review of Bauer's playing, Julius Hartt wrote,

> *No pianist of the period has so steadily and increasingly influenced American musical development. His appeal has never been addressed to the sensation-loving masses. The quiet dignity and fine modesty of an artist too great to exploit himself, and too true to indulge in the theatrical, he has been to a unique degree an artist to artists, a pianist to pianists, a musician to musicians. Only history can award him his proper place in the musical development of the period.*

Moshe Paranov, in his dean's report, May 19, 1936, described Bauer as "a great musician, great teacher, and above all, our loyal and inspiring friend, we owe more than can be told." Throughout the years of World War II, Harold Bauer was an honorary member of the board of trustees for the Julius Hartt School of Music. Bauer's friendship with Moshe Paranov grew very close during those years. The challenges of maintaining a school of music during lean financial war times weighed heavily on everyone involved. Their correspondence reveals that Paranov often confided in Bauer for advice and guidance.

(L–R) Harold Bauer, Moshe Paranov, and Sam Berkman in animated conversation.

of the newly formed Cleveland Institute. Throughout this time he maintained a strong relationship with JHSM. Bloch wrote to Julius Hartt in 1927 saying, *"I have a vague, but certain feeling, that you did not need words from me, to know that I do not change, that I am the same, in spite of all outside happenings, that my heart is the same, my friendship for you the same... that years and distance, and now people have not obliterated dear memories."*

ERNEST BLOCH

In 1917, Julius Hartt met internationally recognized composer Ernest Bloch and introduced him to Morris Perlmutter (Moshe Paranov). Bloch became a valued member of the Hartt family. He came to the United States in 1916 and taught counterpoint, composition, and theory as an associated teacher at the school from 1918 to 1920. He is listed as the artistic director for the Julius Hartt School of Music (JHSM) in The First Catalogue. Julius wrote of him,

66 *For seep [sic] of imagination, emotional eloquence, intellectual grasp, and technical mastery—for these attributes in combination, he has no living equal. His Powers are heaven sent. Revealing technical virtuosity in the highest degree he is not a virtuoso after the manner of many modern composers. Rather with him inspiration is the driving force.*

Bloch lived next door to the JHSM on Collins Street. He moved to Cleveland in 1921 when he became the director

Ernest Bloch
1889-1959

BLOCH, Woodblock by Lucienne Bloch, 1929

Program of Bloch's Sacred Service — A Hartt and Hartford Community tribute to Ernest Bloch, 1959.

UNIVERSITY OF HARTFORD
HARTT SCHOOL OF MUSIC
BETH EL TEMPLE
and
THE JEWISH COMMUNITY CENTER

present

THE SACRED SERVICE
by
Ernest Bloch
1880 - 1959

A Centennial Tribute

Moshe Paranov conducting

The University-Community Chorus & Orchestra

Sunday, April 5, 1981   8:00 p.m.   Beth El Temple
2626 Albany Avenue
West Hartford

One of Bloch's most durable compositions through time was *The Sacred Service*, a festival piece that celebrates life with highly charged musical language. Moshe Paranov called the work "an expression for all mankind and of the goodness of life, not just a little service for one sect."

Paranov's connection to the Beth El Temple spanned most of his lifetime. In 1981 he conducted Bloch's *The Sacred Service* performed by the university and community choruses and orchestra as a centennial tribute to Bloch.

The Ernest Bloch Society was formally organized in 1968 to develop an appreciation of his works and to establish a library of his complete works.

ELIZABETH WARNER-PARANOV

Elizabeth (Libby) Warner-Paranov was born in 1919, in Bridgewater, Connecticut, attended Mount Holyoke College, Columbia University, and received a bachelor of science degree from the Institute of Musical Art of the Juilliard Foundation in 1941 and a bachelor of music degree from the Hartt School of Music in 1943. She studied organ and piano with several instructors, including Moshe Paranov and Harold Bauer. She served as an organist in Hartford area churches. She was a widely acclaimed piano soloist, accompanist, chamber music performer, and teacher, joining the Hartt School of Music piano faculty in 1942.

Elizabeth (Libby) Warner,
dean of the Hartt School of Music, 1966–1983.

(L–R) Irene Kahn, Madelyn Robb, and Libby Warner preparing for a concert.

offered at the University of Hartford. Libby retired in 1983 and was appointed dean emerita of The Hartt School. She married Moshe Paranov after Pauline passed away in 1981. Their home was built in 1929 by actress Katharine Hepburn's father and was owned and maintained by the University of Hartford. Their marriage was highlighted in a *Hartford Monthly* article in 1988.

During her lifetime Libby was highly involved in the Hartford Community. She volunteered her services as accompanist for the Farmington High School choirs and other groups and was highly visible throughout the city. Libby played a key role in the merger of the Hartt School of Music, Hartford Art School, and Hillyer College to create the University of Hartford in 1957. She became assistant dean in 1960 and was promoted to dean in 1966.

Under her leadership, the doctor or musical arts degree program was initiated, the first doctoral program

Moshe and Libby Warner Paranov, 1988.

ESTABLISHMENT OF THE HARTFORD MUSICAL FOUNDATION

In 1934, the same year as the founding of the Hartford Symphony Orchestra, Julius Hartt was instrumental in the founding of the Hartford Musical Foundation, an organization designed to foster the general cause of music and musical education in Connecticut. With the tireless efforts of Martha Blake Walcott, talented pupil of Moshe Paranov and daughter-in-law of the late Senator Frederic C. Walcott, the temporary trustees established by-laws and secured a bank loan for startup expenses. On June 7, 1935, the permanent trustees of the corporation were elected and the foundation assumed ownership and operation of the Julius Hartt Musical Foundation.

In the November 18, 1936, Hartford Musical Foundation minutes, "A reported confusion between the names of the Hartford Musical Foundation and the Hartford School of Music" and the "association between the Foundation and the Julius Hartt School of Music" was noted. In 1936 Julius Hartt retired as director, and the name of the Hartford Musical Foundation was changed to the Julius Hartt Musical Foundation in his honor in 1937.

In 1938 the board purchased the 187 Broad Street property from the Hartford Seminary so that the rapidly growing school had adequate space for its students and programs. The new school property had an auditorium with a stage, a library, and a space where

A brick and the dome from the Julius Hartt College of Music 187 Broad Street, Hartford, Connecticut.

all students and faculty had meals together. At this time, radio, television, and the recording industry were making a significant impact on the curriculum of most educational institutions. The school had 25 faculty and 344 students upon entering the Broad Street building and 113 faculty and 1,829 students upon leaving for the University of Hartford campus in 1963.

Nina Paranov described the Julius Hartt College of Music as a family. *"Mattresses were kept under the piano so students could stay all night and practice any time of the night. When the school bought the 187 Broad Street house in 1938, it was deemed one of the safest buildings in Hartford during the war because of its two basements."* Nina recalled the air raid sirens in Hartford, noting that the state's military industry made Connecticut a perilous place. Because of this, Moshe wouldn't take his family to the beach. Instead, they went to Massachusetts and lived on the lake across from the Tanglewood shed where they could hear the concerts.

Hartt alumni who studied at 187 Broad Street had many fond memories of the building. Al Doty, a 1963 music education and double bass graduate, recalled that the double bass studios were under the front walk of the building where there was actually a space large enough for a classroom. Andrianne Brown, a 1955 music education graduate, recollected that the cello practice room with a full-length mirror was located in

The Julius Hartt College of Music and its dome on 187 Broad Street, Hartford.

Moshe Paranov and Sam Berkman (rear) teaching score analysis

a room just off the girls' restroom, making for some awkward moments getting to their rehearsals. Those who studied there loved the familial environment and their experiences in the grand old building.

At the end of his reports, Paranov always lavishly thanked his faculty, staff, visiting artists, and trustees in inspiring language with variations on these words: *"I am grateful beyond measure to the entire Board of Trustees, to each and every member of the faculty and administrative staff for what they have done and are doing. Their sacrifice and unfailing devotion have made possible our institution as it stands today."* He would then single out individual teaching artists and thank them for their contributions

to the school. Of Harold Bauer, he wrote, *Harold Bauer, the dean of our visiting faculty, and the man whose musical ideals we try to follow, becomes more endeared to us each year. Those of us who come in touch with him and his classes realize that is the greatest single influence in the life of our institution.*

Paranov also addressed the realities of the financial challenges of the school. In his dean's report of the JHSM Trustees in May 19, 1936, he wrote that Julius Hartt's *"ideal and ambition was to make true musicians in every sense of the word. During these years there were many times when it seemed as though our life's ambition would have to be abandoned. But in 1929, despite all our handicaps, we found ourselves financially ready to carry out some of the dreams of Mr. Hartt. Fate seemed to decree otherwise, however, and we, like many others, awoke to find ourselves face to face with one of the worst depressions in history. I am proud to say that because of an overpowering belief in our ideal we were able to keep our doors open during this trying time."*

By 1940, the academic Julius Hartt School of Music had expanded in numerous ways: the student population had grown to nearly 700, the state granted it the right to confer the degree of bachelor of music, the faculty continued to grow, and internationally recognized artists conducted classes: Friedrich Schorr, world-famous singer and leading baritone of the Metropolitan Opera; Dr. Karl Weigl, internationally known composer; William Kroll, violinist and founder of the Coolidge Quartet; and Dr. Alfred Einstein, noted German musicologist. A department of dance had been added. In his May 28, 1940, director's report, Moshe Paranov stated,

66 *Our aim is to turn out well-trained and cultured musicians. After examining very carefully the results our students have achieved and after making a survey of the work done in other musical institutions, we have every reason to be encouraged and proud.*

THE TRUSTEES

OF

THE JULIUS HARTT MUSICAL FOUNDATION

EXTEND TO YOU A CORDIAL

INVITATION TO ATTEND THE

TWENTIETH ANNIVERSARY CELEBRATION

OF THE FOUNDING OF

THE JULIUS HARTT SCHOOL OF MUSIC

TUESDAY EVENING, OCTOBER 22, 1940

AT 8:30 O'CLOCK

THE PROGRAM WILL FEATURE A CONCERT BY FRIEDRICH SCHORR, METROPOLITAN OPERA BARITONE AND NEWLY APPOINTED HEAD OF THE SCHOOL'S VOICE DEPARTMENT; GREETINGS FROM REPRESENTATIVE FIGURES IN THE EDUCATIONAL FIELD; AND AN INSPECTION OF THE SCHOOL'S NEW STUDIO ANNEX.

(Please return your ticket reservation blank at once)

The Twentieth Anniversary program

WORLD WAR II

In acknowledging the extraordinary challenges of World War II, Paranov wrote in his October 29, 1942, board report,

> *In these days of storm and stress we all need to help each other, and by so doing I am sure that not only will we succeed in keeping alive the spirit that makes the Julius Hartt Musical Foundation what it is, but also will we find ourselves as individuals in possession of the rich happiness which invariably comes as a result of doing well as beautiful and necessary work. Many things will be destroyed before this terrible holocaust is over. To what will our youth return? What can be salvaged? What must be salvaged and maintained at cost are the things of the spirit, the things that enable me; and the greatest contributor to the spirit, next to religion, is music. It is our function and great duty to keep this institution alive so that hope and beauty may be experienced again. There is no doubt in my mind that all of us together, with God's help, will reach this noble goal.*

The 1942 academic year brought a first-time decrease in enrollment at the school. The principal causes were the lowering of the draft age to 18 years, the sharp curtailment of the use of private cars for transportation, the difficulties students encountered with public transportation schedules, and the decrease in dollar value of income from the "white collar" group of workers, whose children comprised the majority of the school's enrollment. Though the operations of the school were not dramatically altered, the budgets were. Fund-raising efforts were stepped up so that the educational quality of the school would be maintained. In 1943, the JHMF adopted a new seal for the foundation and the Greek motto, ENEKA TOU KLOU, which means "IN THE SERVICE OF THE BEAUTIFUL." In a speech Paranov warned against institutions that "foster educated automatons rather than well-rounded educated human beings." He went on to say,

> *Those who have chosen art as a life work and who have accepted the motto 'In the Service of the Beautiful,' realize that education must embrace an all-inclusive program if our civilization and democracy are to reach their highest development.*

The logo was created and adopted by the JHMF Board of Trustees in 1950.

As the war raged on, Paranov wrote in his January 26, 1944, director's report,

> *Today, many young men and women are being trained to kill with instruments of destruction. We too, are privileged to train many young men and women, but, thank God, we educate them to understand life and truth and to create with instruments of construction, to create and recreate great music. The world is undergoing great and terrible changes, the like of which man never would have dreamed possible. Men and women are enduring horrors so that we may live with our loved ones a life of peace that we may enjoy, as we see fit, our religion, our music, our painting, our sculpture, and other fine and noble gifts of civilization. It is our sacred duty to preserve our mode of life for the men and women engaged in this terrible Holocaust. I know you who make up the Board which governs the destinies of the JHMF must feel an incomparable satisfaction when you realize you have insisted that this institution must live. You have shared your possessions with your less fortunate brothers. Our continued growth is your ringing and defiant answer to those Satanic tyrants who would destroy our precious heritage, a heritage which comes to us now to illuminate our future paths of service. Let us pray God that we may be permitted to do everything possible that will assure our unwavering progress along these paths, that we many continue always "in the service of the beautiful."*

The 25th anniversary of the Julius Hartt School of Music in 1945 was highlighted by a fund campaign to expand and modernize the 187 Broad Street building. The effort was launched amidst the backdrop of World War II. Not surprisingly, the theme was Music in a Democracy. By this time, the school employed 45 faculty and had more than 900 students.

The 25th anniversary *JHSM Bulletin*

The University of Hartford, 1966.
A completed Hartt College of Music (Fuller) Building
is seen in upper right. The Gengras Student Union is
under construction as is the Barney School of Business
and the administration building.

2 | FORMATION OF THE UNIVERSITY OF HARTFORD

> 66 *Our friends, our community, and the musical world have come to expect great things from us. So far, the Julius Hartt Musical Foundation has never faltered in our responsibility to them and we must not let them down now or at any future time. The rare and indomitable Julius Hartt spirit which seems to permeate the soul of every human being associated with our institution is stronger now than ever before. This light of truth must never be allowed to be extinguished.*
>
> Director's Annual Report to the trustees,
> Moshe Paranov, October 29, 1952

ALFRED C. FULLER

Alfred C. Fuller, who became a member of the board of trustees in 1937, was elected president of the Julius Hartt Music Foundation in 1947. Fuller was nationally recognized as the chairman of the Fuller Brush Company and president of the Manufacturers Association of Connecticut. In June of 1946, Fuller presented plans for the construction of a one-story building and additions to the basement level. But in 1947 Fuller revised his proposal, expanding the construction to include a new auditorium with a theater and concert hall seating about 600 persons. The cost was estimated at $250,000, with Fuller offering to underwrite $100,000 of the total.

In January of 1948 the board announced Fuller's generous gift of $100,000 for the new concert hall and theatre. Construction, however, was delayed due to the potential formation of the University of Hartford. By 1962, Fuller had invested nearly $2 million to create and perpetuate the Hartt College of Music. Though Fuller died in 1973, to this day his generosity is felt and appreciated. Moshe Paranov, in a 1957 board of trustee's report, lavished well-deserved praise on Fuller's contributions to the school.

> *As for my Board of Trustees, without their patience and understanding, this School could never be. Speaking for my entire staff, you have our wholehearted thanks. If any of you think you are harassed by me, there is one man who has proven he can take it! To stand me and my hallucinations, a man must be a super man—brave, with the patience of Job and the skin of an alligator. That man deserves yours and my admiration and love. I present him to you and I am sure I speak for all of you when I say we are forever in his debt for what he is doing for us and humanity, Alfred C. Fuller.*

Alfred Fuller, benefactor of the Alfred C. Fuller Building.

As the plans for creating a university continued to materialize, concerns about maintaining the school's high standards in a university setting arose. In his January 27, 1948, director's report to the JHMF Trustees, Paranov relayed his concerns:

> *Success brings one joy and happiness: It also brings worry in the form of added responsibilities. Since receiving these new honors my Executive Committee and the heads of all departments have met with me daily and have pointed out in no uncertain terms what they consider weaknesses in our set-up and have given me valuable suggestions in order to maintain our very high standards. They will brook no interference in their search for perfection and are determined to keep the Julius Hartt School of Music at the head of the list of music schools in our country.*

When the school prepared for its thirtieth anniversary, Moshe Paranov exclaimed in his annual directors report, "Starting with our 30th year it will no longer be necessary to begin my reports by saying the Julius Hartt School of Music is the finest school in the land—and this has been the most successful year in the school's history." He wrote that everyone now says these things to him. By September 12, 1950, 1,954 students had enrolled in the school.

Internationally acclaimed composers Henry Cowell, Aaron Copland, and Roger Sessions were programmed for the second Institute of Contemporary American

Music (ICAM) series. Edward Diemente, a Hartt graduate, joined the faculty as a piano, theory, and composition teacher. Myra Hess, world famous English pianist, performed with the Hartt Symphony Orchestra at the Bushnell Memorial Hall in 1951 and donated her services so that the school could use the money raised for any desired activity.

The summer program was successfully started. The increase of students, though attributed in part to the influx of veterans supported by the G.I. bill, was met with careful planning rather than "fly-by-night" over-expansion of the school. A differentiation between the junior and adult curricula and the college curriculum was clearly defined. In 1951 the Connecticut State Board of Education approved the bachelor of music education and master of music education degrees. The Connecticut State Legislature passed an act creating the Hartt College of Music, while the Julius Hartt School of Music continued as a nonprofessional school of music.

RABBI A. J. FELDMAN
AND THE JULIUS HARTT MUSICAL FOUNDATION CURRICULUM COMMITTEE

Rabbi Abraham Feldman, leader of Beth Israel Synagogue in Hartford from 1925 to 1977, was an active member of the Hartt Board of Directors after joining the board in 1935. His background in education was notable. Through his leadership, the

Papers and Proceedings of the Music Teachers National Association (MTNA) were first published in Hartford in 1906. Waldo Selden Pratt, a professor at the Hartford Theological Seminary (now the Hartford Seminary Foundation) and the first editor of the *Proceedings*, and Ralph Baldwin, superintendent of the Hartford Public Schools, were leaders of the MTNA. Both were closely tied to Julius Hartt.

Rabbi A. J. Feldman joined the Hartt Board of Directors in 1935.

Rabbi Feldman led an active and productive curriculum committee during his tenure. The committee served as an advisory group to the director in consideration of new appointments to faculty and staff, the library and its expansion program, the building program as it affects curricula, examinations for NASM membership, and for graduate degrees, lecturers, and speakers.

A DIFFICULT BUT NECESSARY DECISION

In his 1953 annual report, Moshe Paranov relayed encouraging news about the school's credibility as an institution. However, he voiced concern that *"we have not $1.00 of endowment; there is not one cent available for research, a pension plan, for sabbatical leaves. We have had no salary [increase] system; out of 80 faculty members only 10 receive $4,000 a year."* He expressed apprehension about the lack of room and auditorium, library, and instructional rooms, as well as an inadequate scholarship fund.

In May of 1956, the JHMF Board of Trustees endorsed the plan of establishing the University of Hartford as a federation of local nonprofit, nonsectarian, non-dormitory institutions. Dr. A. J. Feldman and Stephen Langton, secretary pro tem of the JHMF board, were approved to join Hillyer College representatives John Lee and Ward Duffy as incorporators of the University of Hartford. Paranov wrote that he believed "that such an action will be in the best interests of this great educational and artistic enterprise that we have labored devotedly to build."

The decision to join forces by the Hartford Art School, the Hartt College, and Hillyer College as the new University of Hartford was announced November 15, 1956. The Music and Fine Arts unit, consisting of classrooms, studios, and administration offices, would be part of the new 150-acre campus, recently acquired by Hillyer College. In his November 19, 1957, president's report, Moshe Paranov recounted the chronology [opposite] of the formation of the University of Hartford.

Moshe Paranov points to the future site of Hartt College and the University of Hartford to Alan Wilson, president of Hillyer College, 1956.

Alfred Fuller and Mr. and Mrs. Vincent Coffin preparing to view the Fuller Music Building site, October 11, 1958.

University of Hartford Chronology – Administration

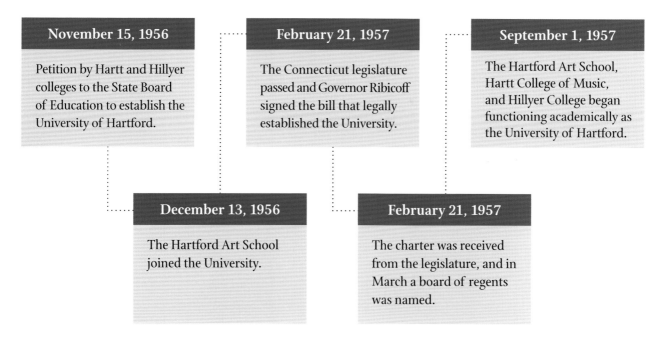

November 15, 1956

Petition by Hartt and Hillyer colleges to the State Board of Education to establish the University of Hartford.

February 21, 1957

The Connecticut legislature passed and Governor Ribicoff signed the bill that legally established the University.

September 1, 1957

The Hartford Art School, Hartt College of Music, and Hillyer College began functioning academically as the University of Hartford.

December 13, 1956

The Hartford Art School joined the University.

February 21, 1957

The charter was received from the legislature, and in March a board of regents was named.

The Administrative Appointments for Hartt College of Music

Hartt College of Music

Moshe Paranov
President

Samuel Berkman
Dean of college

Nathan Gottschalk
Dean of faculty

Pauline H. Paranov
Dean of students

Louis Pellettieri
Dean of admissions

Elizabeth Warner
Assistant dean and registrar

Stephen Langton
Controller

Edward H. Broadhead
Librarian

Julius Hartt School of Music

Moshe Paranov
President

Louis Pellettieri
Director

Madelyn Robb
Assistant director

Elizabeth Warner
Registrar

Stephen Langton
Controller

(L–R) Dean Samuel Berkman, Hartt College of Music; Dr. Alan S. Wilson, President of Hillyer College; Alan Tompkins, director of Hartford Art School; Dr. Moshe Paranov, president of Hartt College of Music, 1966.

Paranov reported,

> *The last twelve months have been the most exciting, breathtaking, stimulating and time-consuming experience in our entire history. Ours has been the almost super-human task of integrating the curricula and policies of three widely divergent institutions. I am proud to tell you that our faculties and administrative officers, along with heads of three colleges, have worked together very harmoniously. In fact, I have never witnessed a group of people who have given of themselves so unstintingly.*

One hundred and fifty Hartford citizens who were chosen from the fields of industry, business, insurance, banking, and other walks of life represented the Founders of the University of Hartford. The funds that were targeted for constructing additions and repairs to the Broad Street school were abandoned when forming the University of Hartford became a serious consideration. The 1962–1963 academic year was the last year the Julius Hartt School of Music and Hartt College of Music resided at 187 Broad Street. While the prospect of leaving their home was difficult to accept, Paranov encouraged everyone to look forward to a new *"sound-proofed, air-conditioned building with 44 studios and practice rooms; 14 academic and administrative offices; 28 faculty offices; four rooms for musical instruments and storage; an observation and recording room, conference facilities; student and faculty lounges; a technical music library, a large rehearsal hall, and a musical theater."*

The 187 Broad Street building was demolished in 1964 to make way for Interstate I-84, "the east-west highway." A parent group of the Julius Hartt School of Music gathered bricks from the building and used them in a fund-raising drive for scholarships and equipment. Donors of five dollars or more received a certificate entitling them to a commemorative, inscribed brick from the old Hartt building.

It was at this time that the Julius Hartt School of Music was recognized by Northwestern Life Insurance Company as one of the "18 Famous American Schools of Music."

Comedian Jack Benny appeared on February 26, 1962, with the Hartt College of Music Symphony Orchestra in the Bushnell Auditorium as part of a fund-raising effort for the school's new facilities. He performed his hilarious sketch "The World's Greatest Violinist" for the occasion.

Marian Anderson leading the singing for a formal dedication of the Alfred C. Fuller Music Center, December 5, 1963.

BUILDING THE UNIVERSITY OF HARTFORD

The formal dedication of the Alfred C. Fuller Music Center, which housed both the Hartt College of Music and the Julius Hartt School of Music, began with an academic program on December 5, 1963, featuring famed singer Marian Anderson. In a 2018 interview, Nina Paranov Fagan recalled the dedication ceremonies of Millard Auditorium in 1964. Nina drove Marian Anderson around town in her "little old Chevy" and described Anderson as very humble with "no delusions of grandeur."

A celebratory concert was presented on December 12, 1963, with guest artists Isaac Stern and Leonard Rose.

Comedian Jack Benny (center, top/bottom) with Chancellor Coffin (top L) and Moshe Paranov (top R), and Primrose and Alfred Fuller, February, 1962.

(L–R) Moshe Paranov, Isaac Stern, and Leonard Rose have a pre-concert chat, December 12, 1963.

Arnold Franchetti's *Psalm VIII for Chorus and Orchestra* was also performed by the Hartt Chorale and Chorus, Philip Treggor, conductor.

In the early years of the university a large amphitheater–music shell was planned in between the Hartt College of Music and the Hartford Art School.

In 1966, Libby Warner was appointed dean of the Hartt College of Music and Samuel Berkman assumed the post of dean emeritus in residence. In 1967 Archibald Woodruff was appointed president of the University of Hartford, and Nathan Gottschalk, who joined the Hartt faculty in 1956, was executive director of Hartt College.

Charter Day, 1966: (L–R) Moshe Paranov, Samuel Berkman, Stephen Langton, William McIlroy, Louis Pellettieri. (L–R) Helen Hubbard, Irene Kahn, Rose Kleeman, Virginia Schorr. *Photograph: Capitol Studios, Inc.*

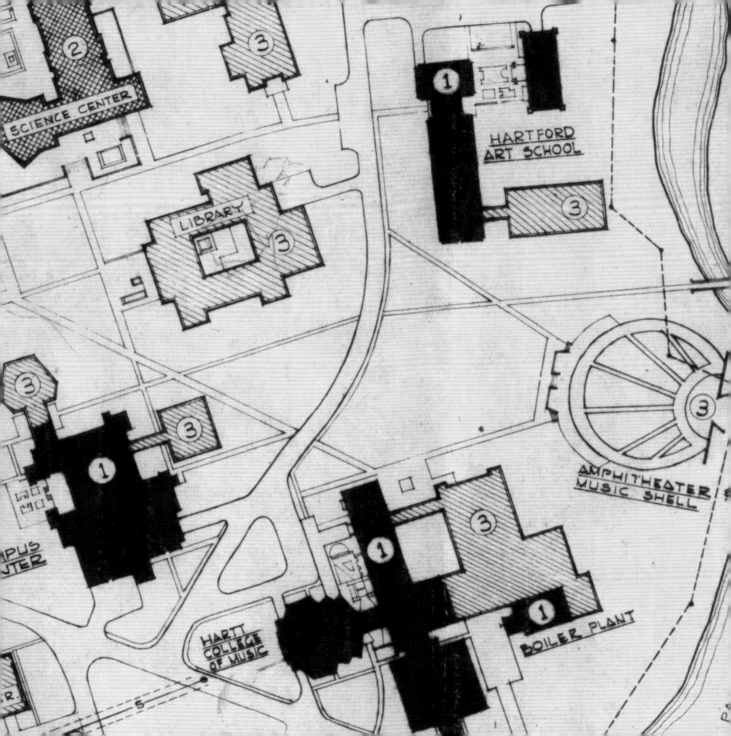

THE FIFTIETH ANNIVERSARY

Mary Primrose Fuller, wife of Alfred C. Fuller, and Martha Blake Walcott were presented honorary doctorates in November of 1970 as part of the Fiftieth Anniversary celebrations. Mrs. Fuller was very active in the Hartford community, including work with the Hartford Symphony Society and the Hartt Opera-Theater Guild. Mrs. Walcott was instrumental in the formation of the Julius Hartt Musical Foundation.

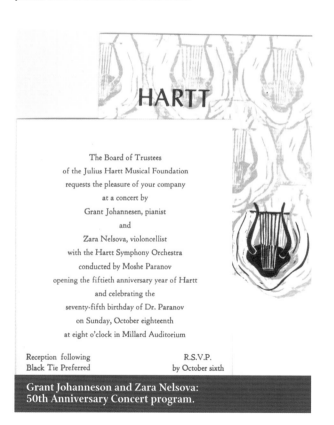

The Board of Trustees
of the Julius Hartt Musical Foundation
requests the pleasure of your company
at a concert by
Grant Johannesen, pianist
and
Zara Nelsova, violoncellist
with the Hartt Symphony Orchestra
conducted by Moshe Paranov
opening the fiftieth anniversary year of Hartt
and celebrating the
seventy-fifth birthday of Dr. Paranov
on Sunday, October eighteenth
at eight o'clock in Millard Auditorium

Reception following   R.S.V.P.
Black Tie Preferred   by October sixth

**Grant Johanneson and Zara Nelsova:
50th Anniversary Concert program.**

Pianist Grant Johanneson and cellist Zara Nelsova performed with the Hartt Symphony Orchestra in October of 1970. In the spring of 1971 The Hartt School presented a special Fiftieth Anniversary concert with Pinchas Zukerman, violin, Eugenia Zukerman, flute, Raymond Hanson and Anne Koscielny, pianists, and the Hartt Chamber Orchestra, Vytautas Marijosius conducting.

Leonard Rose and Issac Stern returned to the Hartt School of Music on April 25, 1971 to celebrate Paranov's 75th birthday and the school's 50th anniversary with an all-Brahms concert. Because of the large audience, the concert was moved to the new Hall High School auditorium in West Hartford. Rose and Stern were presented honorary doctorates from the University of Hartford. Moshe Paranov retired on June 30, 1971, and Donald Mattran, conductor of the Hartt Symphonic Wind Ensemble, director of the Hartt College summer session, and associate professor of conducting and music education at Hartt, became the acting head of the college. Libby Warner remained as dean of Hartt College of Music.

Aaron Copland also returned to conduct the Hartt Symphony Orchestra for his 70th birthday. The concert included two of his works, and those of Diemente, Putsché, and Franchetti. Copland had recently been appointed to Hartt's National Executive Board.

Aaron Copland conducts the Hartt Symphony Orchestra to celebrate his 70th birthday and Moshe's 75th birthday.

Koussevitsky, and composer-conductors Leonard Bernstein and Aaron Copland were named to the newly formed National Executive Committee of the Hartt College of Music. The committee was established during the 50th anniversary for the purpose of advising Hartt officials in the development of national programming and fund-raising for the second half-century of the institution.

CIVIL UNREST

Events of the late 1960s and early 1970s had a great impact on Hartt College and the University of Hartford campus as they did nationwide. The escalation of the war in Vietnam, the invasion of Cambodia, the shooting of innocent college students at Kent State, and the inequities of race and gender profoundly moved students and civilians to protest and openly call for change. A massive demonstration resulted in damage to the Gengras Campus Center. The university worked to honor students' concerns by holding open forums and encouraging full participation by all in the events arranged by students and faculty. The university remained open during this time, but provided opportunities for dealing with the civil turmoil among the university community. The university invited speakers Malcolm X (1963), Jerry Rubin (1967), Julian Bond (1969), and Timothy Leary (1977).

The school had experienced impressive growth since its meager beginnings in 1920. New programs that reflected the changing needs and tastes of the country were started during this fifty-year period of birth and growth. In 1971 Marian Anderson, Mrs. Serge

At a meeting on May 5, 1970, attended by members of the Student Senate, the Faculty Senate, and academic deans and administration, recommendations were formulated to deal with the remainder of the school year. Students were given the option of attending any or all classes and taking examinations as dictated by their own conscience. Students could opt for pass/fail grades. The Student Senate voted unanimously to support the nationwide student strike on May 6. African American students presented a 19-point proposal, which included items such as scholarships for black athletes, the universal observance of black holidays, and that the matriculated students should reflect the black ethnic percentage of Hartford. The university set up a task force of faculty and black students to explore the issues and submit proposed solutions.

The Symphonic Wind Ensemble concert scheduled that month was canceled. Rallies and speeches were organized. A memorial scholarship fund in honor of slain Kent State students was established. Peter Woodard, a Hartt student at the time, recalled that the Vietnam War profoundly affected the interactions between teachers and students. For example, Jackie McLean regularly opened up the class for students to discuss their thoughts and reactions to incidents such as the Jackson State killings before addressing the class assignments.

Several JHMF trustees at the May 25, 1970, meeting reported that university students were not upset with their schools but were demonstrating as "a humanistic act of moral rebellion." Despite the unrest, attendance at Hartt was about 97 percent, which was about the normal average.

In April 1972, students, faculty, and staff together held a strike on the university campus. Imanuel Willheim and Arnold Franchetti presented a speech on revolution, Nazism, and Fascism to the Hartt students as part of a rally. One student asked how to start a revolution, to which Willheim patted Franchetti on the back and said, "Let's do it!" In the same year, 18-year-olds were allowed to vote, and their voices continue to make an impact.

THE HARTT SCHOOL – A VISUAL HISTORY

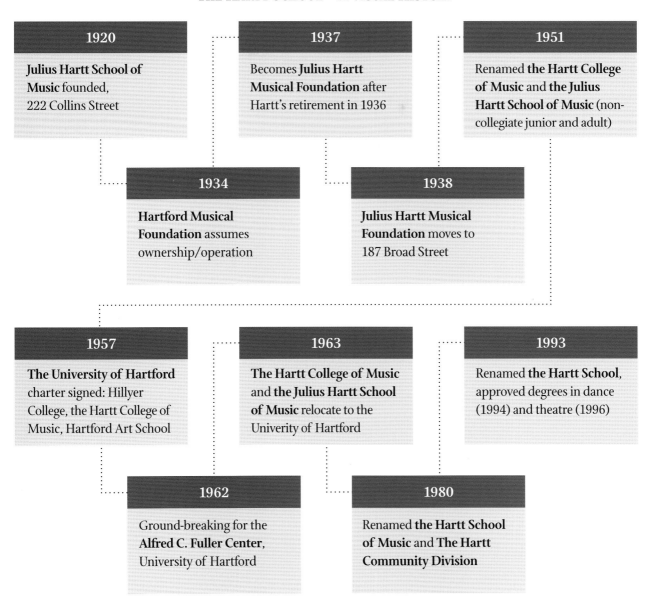

1920

Julius Hartt School of Music founded, 222 Collins Street

1937

Becomes **Julius Hartt Musical Foundation** after Hartt's retirement in 1936

1951

Renamed **the Hartt College of Music** and **the Julius Hartt School of Music** (non-collegiate junior and adult)

1934

Hartford Musical Foundation assumes ownership/operation

1938

Julius Hartt Musical Foundation moves to 187 Broad Street

1957

The University of Hartford charter signed: Hillyer College, the Hartt College of Music, Hartford Art School

1963

The Hartt College of Music and **the Julius Hartt School of Music** relocate to the Univerity of Hartford

1993

Renamed **the Hartt School**, approved degrees in dance (1994) and theatre (1996)

1962

Ground-breaking for the **Alfred C. Fuller Center**, University of Hartford

1980

Renamed **the Hartt School of Music** and **The Hartt Community Division**

3 | THE HARTT SCHOOL COMMUNITY DIVISION

> 66 *We are a miniature college with roots deeply embedded in the educational, musical, and cultural life of the Greater Hartford area.*
>
> Louis Pelletieri, director of the
> Julius Hartt School of Music

From its inception in 1920, the Julius Hartt School of Music (JHSM) was founded as a music teaching program serving the greater Hartford community. The JHSM offered an in-depth educational program that embraced every aspect of music study for young people and adults, including all phases of private and class instruction in instruments, voice, and theoretical subjects, but also experiences in orchestras, bands, choruses, chamber music, stage productions, and recitals. Faculty taught collegiate classes when they began in 1927 as well as classes for the School of Music. Over time the school expanded to include

classes in theatre and dance through community partnerships. The faculty's dedication to the highest teaching standards and artistic ideas in both the academic and nonacademic areas are recognized nationally and internationally.

Music lessons for children, Julius Hartt School of Music, 1950–51.

LOUIS J. PELLETTIERI

Louis J. Pellettieri, a student of Julius Hartt, served as the admissions director and taught music history, piano, and choral conducting at the Julius Hartt School of Music. He was appointed the school's director beginning in 1937 and continued this role in 1957, when the school joined the University of Hartford. Pellettieri founded the Greater Hartford Community Chorus in 1963 and conducted many choral organizations, including choirs from the Mount Saint Joseph Academy and the Wethersfield Women's Chorus in the 1940s.

Louis Pelletieri, director of the Julius Hartt School of Music, 1937–1974. *Photo by John Vignoli*

In a report to the University of Hartford Regents in November 1969, Pelletieri began by assuring the Regents that Hartt College of Music and the Julius Hartt School of Music were not one and the same. The generic term "Hartt" is, he wrote, *"like the Traveler's umbrella, which covers two distinct schools—one on the collegiate level, the other on the non-collegiate junior and adult level."* He compared Hartt to other professional, conservatory-type music schools such as the Eastman School of Music, the New England Conservatory, and Juilliard, noting their preparatory divisions serve the needs of pre-college-age students and adults.

> 66 *The JHSM is virtually the preparatory division of Hartt College. The training of musicians begins then, not at the college level, but at the pre-school and elementary school levels. I came to Hartt as a student in 1927 at the recommendation of the late Ralph Baldwin, who was then supervisor of Music in the Hartford Public Schools. My association with Hartt as student, teacher, and administrator covers a span of 42 years. I have had the honor of working under the dynamic and inspiring leadership of Moshe Paranov, who infected me with an incurable virus called Harttitis. My admiration for him as a musician and above all as a human being is boundless. He firmly believes that Hartt College and the Julius Hartt School of Music are the greatest schools in the world. And so do I!*

GROWTH OF THE JULIUS HARTT SCHOOL OF MUSIC

Between 1934 and 1942 Alwin Nicholais led the first dance instruction at the school. Advertisements were placed in local papers for modern dance and ballet classes at the 187 Broad Street location. The school continued to offer nonprofessional classes through the war years of the 1940s. Elemer Nagy's opera program involved students in both programs characterized by the fluid involvement of the faculty and instructors in the collegiate and noncollegiate programs. By 1940, the Julius Hartt School of Music became the first independent institution in the state to confer a bachelor of music degree, and in 1942 the State Board of Education granted approval for the school to offer music education courses. In 1951 the Connecticut State Legislature passed an act creating the Hartt College of Music, while the Julius Hartt School of Music continued as a school of music on the nonprofessional level.

THE HARTT SCHOOL TRAINING ORCHESTRA

Multiple community orchestras emerged over time. The Hartt School Training Orchestra began in 1938 with ten students, ages 11–16, and was directed by Rubin Segal, chair of the string department until his death in 1955. Vytautas Marijosius and Nathan Gottschalk succeeded Segal as directors of the orchestra. Over the decades, scores of former members of the orchestra, renamed the Hartford Youth Orchestra in the 1950s, have held important positions with major symphony orchestras around the country. The purpose of the organization from the beginning was to foster character building as well as good musicianship. The young participants learned to shoulder and carry out responsibilities, to attend all rehearsals, and to give their best efforts.

The 1960s saw a tremendous increase in program offerings. In addition to instruction in harp and dance

Early JHSM Training Orchestras, Rubin Segal, conductor.

featured in the Junior and Adult Divisions, the Suzuki Violin Method (3–12) was introduced in 1967. The Junior and Adult programs grew from 100 students in 1920 to 2,000 students in 1969. In 1963 the budget was $190,000 and in 1968, $335,000. In 1965 the school focused on enhancing the Adult Division as well as increasing scholarship funds. A "Friends of the Julius Hartt School of Music Scholarship Fund" was formulated.

GREATER HARTFORD COMMUNITY CHORUS

In 1963 Louis Pelletieri formed the Greater Hartford Community Chorus, which brought together over 100 amateur adult singers from over twenty communities in the Greater Hartford area. From its beginnings the chorus performed major works, including a memorable performance of Felix Mendelssohn's *Elijah*

Rehearsal accompanyist (L) joins Joan Glazier, Phyllis Stoltz, and Howard Sprout in preparing for the 1974 performance of Vivaldi's *Gloria*.

Louis Pelletieri conducting *Elijah* with Arthur Thompson in the title role, March 25, 1972.

on March 25, 1972. The performance featured Hartt graduate Arthur Thompson, a member of New York's Metropolitan Opera Studio, who sang the title role along with another celebrated opera singer and Hartt alumnus, Esther Hinds Brown.

In December of 1974, Robert Christensen, then director of the JHSM, conducted Vivaldi's *Gloria* with Joan Glazier, Phyllis Stoltz, and Hartt graduate Howard Sprout.

The 1970 summer session brochure included a statement expressing the program's educational objectives: *To discover and train the gifted and to provide quality instruction and musical experiences for the large segment of young people and adults not destined for the professional field.* At the Fuller Music Building on the University of Hartford campus, as at the Broad Street location, the collegiate and noncollegiate divisions shared the building, facilities, library, and distinguished teachers on the college faculty. Also in the 1970s Tanya Paranov directed the Children's Workshop (pre-k) and Singing School (4–12). Children in the Singing School received specialized training in group and solo singing as well as preparation for performance in the JHSM and Hartt College opera productions, including Humperdinck's *Hansel and Gretel, The Little Sweep* (Benjamin Britten), *Johnny Appleseed* (Carmino Ravosa), and *Who Are the Blind* (Mary Lynn Trombly, a Hartt College alumna).

Hartt alumnus Joseph Mulready served as director of the Summer School in 1973, and Gerald Mack assumed direction of the Hartt Chorus, which had performed to rave reviews at the Chicago Convention of Music Educators National Conference (MENC).

In the 1980s Bernard Lurie, concertmaster of the Hartford Symphony Orchestra (HSO) and member of the Hartt College string faculty, conducted the Greater Hartford Youth Orchestra (GHYO) that included 85 high-school-age musicians representing 30 communities around the Hartford area. In 1980 the Hartt College of Music was renamed the Hartt School of Music, and the Julius Hartt School of Music became the Hartt Community Division (HCD). New bylaws were established for the GHYO orchestra in 1982, assuring its organizational structure into the future.

Tanya Paranov, director of the JHSM Children's Workshop and Singing School.

(L–R) Bernard Lurie, conductor of the Greater Hartford Youth Orchestra (GHYO), Julius Cremisis, president of the GHYO Association, and Donald Harris, dean of the Hartt School of Music, 1982.

SATELLITES

Satellite locations were established to extend the services of the Community Division. Simsbury was the first community to open a facility, with its ribbon-cutting on September 4, 1984, and an enrollment 67. Arthur Levine headed the Simsbury program, and Al Lepak, acclaimed percussionist, agreed to do a fund-raising concert to benefit the program. Lenzy Wallace Jr. was director of the Hartt Community Division (1981–1984) at that time. Donald Harris, dean of The Hartt School, noted that interest in the Special Music Education Program (SMEP) was increasing, and the visual arts were added as a new component. In the JHSM graduation exercises, diplomas, certificates, awards, and prizes were traditionally awarded to students old and young.

Michael Yaffe, director of the Community Division; associate dean of The Hartt School, 1986–2006.

In the 1980s Moshe Paranov had served as a guest conductor in local school districts. In Glastonbury, Larry D. Allen, director of music, invited Moshe to develop an artist-in-residence program that involved several components. Moshe visited the schools one day per month with a full-day program of concerts, master classes, and lectures.

Because the focus of the program was to collaborate with various language classes (including English, Spanish, French, German, and Russian), performers from the Hartt School of Music came to the school to play the music and discuss the cultures of the class students were taking. Among the faculty were pianist Luis de Mauro Castro, who spoke seven languages and frequently shared information and music with the German, Russian, and French classes. Other notable faculty included Bert Lucarelli, oboe, and Libby Warner, accompanist on piano; Peter Harvey, vocal soloist and historian; and Gary Karr, contrabass. In addition to the original faculty, jazz musician Jackie McLean, founder of the Hartt jazz program, and Richard Provost, founder of The Hartt School guitar program offered performances to school children.

In 1986 Michael Yaffe was appointed director of the Community Division. He came to Hartt from the staff of the National Association of Schools of Music with a mandate from Dean Donald Harris to make the program a contemporary community arts school with high-quality instruction in all areas.

While the Community Division of that era had strong attributes, it also was losing money. Some of the best regional music teachers had chosen to teach on their own or through the two other community schools in the region, the Hartford Conservatory and the Camerata School of Music and Dance. As a result, Yaffe developed a strategic direction during his first year at Hartt. The focus of that initial work was to ensure that quality teaching was occurring at all levels of the division and that the reinvigoration of the Community Division would begin with early childhood, which would provide a pipeline of students through high school. He focused on reviewing the quality of teaching and appointed new faculty members in many areas of the school.

As part of the "pipeline" in 1987, Teri and David Einfeldt joined the Community Division as full-time staff members to lead the Suzuki program. In partnership with the Music Education Department of The Hartt School, John Feierabend, an expert in early childhood music education, was brought to Hartford to teach music education and also to create the Connecticut Center for Early Childhood in Music and Movement. These three appointments set new high standards for the Community Division, since they were each national leaders in their respective fields. In addition, Yaffe appointed two ensembles in residence to encourage the performance of chamber music and to add new faculty in winds and brass: The Brass Ring brass quintet and the Soni Fidelis Woodwind Quintet formed the basis of a new set of faculty members in those areas.

A long-range plan was created in 1992–93 with a threefold mission:

- To serve as a training school for precollege musicians with career aspirations and/or exceptional musical talent

- To function as a program that provides a variety of music instruction at varying levels for as many youngsters as possible and to further serve as a complement for home school music programs

- To serve as a resource for adults with amateur interests in music

RECOGNITION
A NATIONAL REPUTATION

With the 1987 national appointments and many others locally, the Hartt Community Division became known in Hartford and nationally as one of the most prestigious community arts schools in the country. The work of the Community Division was recognized as a model for community music schools in the context of universities. Through time, many teachers in the Community Division have prepared performers for the best music schools in the country. Literally hundreds of Community Division students work in orchestras, music faculty positions, chamber music groups, and other music activities today. In the 1990s the Performer's Certificate program, honors recitals, and other recognition activities were created to honor outstanding performers. At the same time, many students in that period simply wanted good music instruction with no career aspirations. That balance continues to this day.

By 1991, the Community Division saw impressive growth. Student numbers topped 2,500, and the number of teachers expanded to 125. In addition, over twenty teachers of the Community Division became fully employed by the University of Hartford. The Hartt Suzuki program expanded in both numbers and stature thanks to the Enfield's vision, including a summer Hartt Suzuki Institute, four Suzuki orchestras, teaching in violin, viola, cello, piano, and guitar, and the development of a graduate program in Suzuki pedagogy in collaboration with the Hartt School. In that year, John Feierabend was awarded the prestigious LEGO prize.

The large ensemble programs were also expanded during and after this period to include the Connecticut Youth Symphony and the Greater Hartford Youth Wind Ensemble for high school instrumentalists, the Connecticut Children's Chorus, the Concert Orchestra, and the Young People's Orchestra. These, combined with an expanded presence of chamber music, made the Community Division a comprehensive music school for children ages birth to eighteen as well as adults. During that time, a New Horizons Band for adults was developed, along with private lesson programs and concerts designed specifically for adult amateurs.

Hartt received accreditation first through the Non-Degree Granting Commission of NASM in the early 1990s (now defunct) and beginning in 2000 through the Accrediting Commission of Community and Pre-Collegiate Arts Schools. Hartt was one of the first schools at that time to receive both non-degree-granting and degree-granting accreditation.

Dan D'Addio, director, Connecticut Youth Symphony.

During the 1990s the ensemble program experienced significant growth and restructuring. The Greater Hartford Youth Orchestra was renamed the Connecticut Youth Symphony, and the youth wind ensemble programs transitioned to a premiere performance ensemble known as Greater Hartford Youth Wind Ensemble.

CONNECTICUT YOUTH SYMPHONY

After years of successful leadership of the wind ensemble program, conductor and Hartt alumnus Daniel D'Addio took the helm of the state's leading youth orchestra, the Connecticut Youth Symphony, in 2001. During his 20-plus year tenure, D'Addio led the performance organization to an exciting high, fostering concerto competitions, guest artists, engagement of new music opportunities, collaborations, and an overall growth in the level of repertoire and preparation.

GREATER HARTFORD YOUTH WIND ENSEMBLE

With D'Addio's appointment to the Connecticut Youth Symphony, the leadership of Greater Hartford Youth Wind Ensemble was entrusted to Glen Adsit, newly appointed director of bands for The Hartt School. The ensemble continued its growth and reputation-enhancement in the region, serving as an outlet for advanced high school winds, brass, and percussion students. During the early 2000s both CYS

The Greater Hartford Youth Wind Ensemble in rehearsal, Glen Adsit, conductor.

and GHYWE worked collaboratively on many fronts, including tours and regional presentations that brought national recognition to the ensembles.

The Suzuki program was greatly expanded in the late 1980s by Teri and David Einfeldt. Suzuki programming advanced in instruments offered, group instruction, and a Suzuki orchestra model. To provide year-round opportunities in the greater Hartford area, the Einfeldts founded the Hartt Suzuki Institute, a weeklong summer workshop for children as well as teachers. David Einfeldt, who directed the Suzuki string orchestra and taught Suzuki viola, passed away suddenly and unexpectedly in 1996. Immediately following his death, family, friends, students, and colleagues from across the country established a fund in David's honor which has supported the program's growth and development for years. Teri Einfeldt has continued to shape and build a program, which is considered a national model, fostering educational opportunities for students from birth to adult, including a long-term training program at the graduate level. A significant number of HCD's valuable Suzuki faculty are graduates of The Hartt School's graduate emphasis in Suzuki pedagogy program.

In May of 1992, the Opus '89 String Orchestra, founded in 1987 by David Einfeldt, was the only large student ensemble to be invited to perform at the International Suzuki Teacher Conference in Chicago. This prestigious

Teri and David Einfeldt, Suzuki String Program, Hartt Community Division.

string orchestra performs advanced repertoire and has toured internationally and is now led by Hartt alumnus Emmett Drake.

CAPITOL SYMPHONIC WINDS

In the early 1990s, a growing demand for a high-level adult ensemble experiences spurred the creation of Capitol Symphonic Winds, an idea conceived by Hartt alumnus Neal Smith. The ensemble, which consists of local music educators, university students, and auditioned instrumentalist from the larger community, was led for 23 years by local conductor and prominent music educator Gary Partridge. During his tenure, Partridge grew the ensemble from a small collection of two dozen players to over 90 accomplished musicians, becoming a Hartford "must see" high-quality wind ensemble. After Partridge's retirement in 2018, Dr. Daniel D'Addio assumed the leadership of this important organization.

A TEMPORARY HOME
Suzuki String Program

During the early 2000s, in response to continued demands for growth, the Hartt Community Division established a partnership with the West Hartford Universalist Church on Fern Street to create a temporary home for the popular Suzuki String Program (with daunting waitlists on multiple instruments). Within a 15-year period, the large space became home to over 350 Suzuki string families, filling the building to capacity, Monday through Friday only. The HCD continues to explore options for a more permanent space solution that would allow for additional growth.

CREATING WORLD-CLASS ARTISTS AND PERFORMERS

The Community Division remains a haven for the region's most-talented performing artists. Students have flocked to the school to study with renowned and proven instructors, who produce high school graduates attending such world-class conservatories as Curtis, Juilliard, The Hartt School, the Eastman School, Jacob's School of Music, and the Thornton School of Music. Other organizations have hired graduates in top orchestra leadership roles, including the Minnesota Orchestra, the Los Angeles Philharmonic, and many others. Although a vast majority of HCD graduates do not pursue the performing arts at the college level, many minored in these areas and establish themselves as high-level achievers, thinkers, and contributors in their respective disciplines.

NEW SIMSBURY SATELLITE
The Yakemore Family Performing Arts Center

In October of 2003, Andrew Yakemore and then director Michael Yaffe worked closely together to establish a center for high-quality arts education in Simsbury. The former Simsbury Satellite was moved into a state-of-the-art facility at Simsmore Square, a location outfitted and built by the Yakemore family, under special arrangement with The Hartt Community Division. Yakemore's love of the performing arts and the family's dedication to a home and foundation for arts education led to a ten-studio, two sprung-floor movement studio Yakemore Family Performing Arts Center.

SCHOOL SATELLITES

In addition to established facilities on the university's main campus, Fern Street in West Hartford, and the Simsmore Square Satellite, Director Michael Yaffe saw great promise in the growth and development of partnerships with local schools. These carefully organized relationships brought high-quality private lessons to the students in a convenient way that fostered strong synergies with the schools. Locations included Glastonbury Public Schools, the Kingswood Oxford School, Middletown Public Schools, the Renbrook School, South Windsor, and others.

FUND FOR ACCESS

Since the early 1990s access to performing arts education has remained at the forefront of the Community Division's mission. Major fund-raising initiatives established the school's Fund for Access program, which deployed need-based financial aid to the region's most-deserving students whose families could not otherwise afford HCD's life-changing educational programming. Annually, the Fund for Access awarded over $100,000 in need-based aid to over 100 young performing artists from nearly 30 towns from across greater Hartford. The need for aid, the reduction of in-school performing arts programming, and the proven transformative impacts of performing arts education continue to propel this important initiative.

CONNECTICUT CHILDREN'S CHORUS

During the 1992–93 academic year, John Feierabend, director of The Hartt School's Music Education program, established a residency with renowned composer, arranger, and educator Doreen Rao. As part of Rao's time at Hartt, Feierabend initiated a children's chorus to serve as a laboratory/training choir for educators. It was apparent that there was a need and desire for a rigorous, diverse, and focused youth choral program in greater Hartford. The early choir of nearly 60 children continued past Rao's residency to become the Connecticut Children's Chorus (CCC). Under the guidance and leadership of founding directors Robert Hugh and the late Sallie Ferrebee, the organization grew from one choir of 60 children to seven graded choirs (grades 1–12) with over 200 students. After Hugh's tenure, the organization was led by Stuart Younse and Ferrebee. Currently,

CCC is directed by a collaborative of the region's top music educators, led by Hartt graduate and CCC inaugural choir alumna Meredith Neumann. CCC tours national and internationally on a biannual schedule, has performed on the *Today Show*, and was named the official Children's Chorus of the Hartford Symphony Orchestra. They perform regularly as guests of the Hartford Chorale, the Berkshire Choral Festival, and participate in other regional performance engagements to great acclaim. Numerous choruses for all ages are offered through the Community Division as well.

DANCE AT THE HARTT SCHOOL COMMUNITY DIVISION

With the closure of Hartford Ballet and the School of Hartford Ballet, the community experienced a great loss of high-quality dance education programming. The School of Dance Connecticut (the successor to the Hartford Ballet) was established to ensure the continuity of instruction. In 2002–3, as Dance Connecticut was closing, administration from the University of Hartford, Dean Larry Alan Smith, Michael Yaffe, and Dance Connecticut board member and JHMF trustee Tracy Flater, among others, worked to save the School of Dance Connecticut as a unit of the Hartt Community Division. Thanks to funding from the Hartford Foundation for Public Giving, the School became the Dance Department of the Community Division, maintaining a presence on Farmington Avenue in Hartford until the move to the Handel Performing Arts Center in 2008. Michael Yaffe described this merger with great pride, saying that it not only saved an exemplary dance program for the region at the time, but it also allowed the Community Division to mirror the artistic expansion of The Hartt School. In 2006, Yaffe was appointed associate dean at the Yale School of Music, leaving a distinguished legacy of service and leadership at The Hartt School and The Hartt Community Division.

Today's Community Division dance program focuses on a vibrant high-level classical ballet program, which annually provides bright young dancers to major companies and schools across the globe. Classes are offered for Pre-K, Classical, Youth, Adult, and summer study. Dance leaders have included Enid Lynn, Susan Brooker, Miguel Campenaria, Samantha Dunster, Carol Roderick, and Sarkis Kaltakchian.

HARTT PREPARATORY ACADEMY

On the heels of a vastly successful Performer's Certificate Program, in 2017 HCD director Noah Blocker-Glynn led the creation of the Hartt Preparatory Academy to continue enhancing an intensive and rigorous academic college preparation program. With approval by the University of Hartford and The Hartt School, the Hartt Preparatory Academy was established to offer the first-year college core curriculum over two years to HCD juniors and seniors. Students who successfully complete the Hartt Preparatory Academy program, audition, and are accepted to the University of Hartford and The Hartt School are eligible for a reduced college degree program (three year degree, major dependent). The program fosters a continuity of study and provides incentive to talented HCD students for study at The Hartt School. This extensive articulation between a preparatory and college-degree-granting program is the first of its kind in the nation.

100 Years of Hartt Community Division Directors	
1920 – 1936	Julius Hartt and Moshe Paranov
1937 – 1974	Louis Pelletieri
1981 – 1984	Lenzy Wallace
1986 – 2006	Michael Yaffe
2007 – 2009	Mark George
2010 – 2015	Hilary Field Respass
2015 – present	Noah Blocker-Glynn

HARTT COMMUNITY DIVISION TODAY (2019)

Following Michael Yaffe's tenure as the HSD director, Mark George became director from 2007 to 2009, appointed by Malcolm Morrison. Dean Aaron Flagg tapped Hilary Field Respass to the position in 2010. Since 2015, The Hartt Community Division has been led by its seventh director, Noah Blocker-Glynn. Blocker-Glynn joined the HCD in 2008 as the events and program coordinator. Under his leadership the Community Division continues to advance distinguished leaders in music, theatre, and dance. As the HCD reaches its centennial, the programs reflect a dedication to the highest teaching standards and artistic ideas that prevailed through the last century.

In addition to the previously noted programs, the HCD offers countless programs for early childhood, youth, and adults in Music, Dance, and Theatre during the school and in the summer. Summer Programming includes many youth programs including the Hartt Suzuki Institute that fills Hartt's halls with string players and guitar for all ages.

The Community Division enters the next century of its life with a solid foundation. More than 90 percent of the faculty have masters degrees or higher. The average length of their service is nineteen years. In 2018 the student population grew to 2,852 with a budget of $3.9 million. The staff and faculty are impassioned believers in its newly honed vision and culture statements that were written to perpetuate the enduring legacy of the HCD.

Teachers in action (L–R) Maggie Francis, Nancy Andersen, and Alan Francis, and Director Noah Blocker-Glynn. *Photographs: Kevin Andersen*

Community Division Programs

- Chamber music programs for adults and children, including Philharmonia Winds and Harmony Winds conducted by Alan Francis; Virtuosi, conducted by Paul Pierce; and Sinfonia and Stringendo, conducted by David Kramer

- Early Childhood Programs including First Steps in Music, led today by Hartt alumna Connie Greenwood

- Prism Project and Adaptive Learning for students with exceptionalities, founded in 2017 and led by Hartt alumna Jackie Smith, who also teaches private lessons

- Guitar Orchestra, directed by David Madsen

- Suzuki string orchestras

- Jazz and Popular Music Institute

- Creative Studies Program including Rock, Roots, and Jazz, songwriting, composition and theory private lessons, a young composer's project, musicianship group classes, conducting basics program, and Chinese music traditions

HCD Summer Programs

- Meet the Masters

- Classical Voice (Vocal Audition Advantage)

- Music Industry

- Summer Musical Theatre Intensive Pre-professional

- Hartt Summer Youth Festival

- Chamber Music Accord

VISION: *By engaging the region's best, most innovative faculty and investing in their continued development, we build an unparalleled educational experience and environment that will enrich the lives of our students regardless of age, background, or level. We are committed to the development of the whole artist through a complement of instruction, collaboration, performance, outreach, and creative exploration.*

CULTURE STATEMENT: *As the community extension of The Hartt School, The Hartt School Community Division further defines its core values as: a commitment to excellence in a warm, friendly, nurturing, inclusive, and diverse environment for all—students, faculty, families, and administration. Our ideals of respect, dignity, personal enrichment, and a professional approach are at the foundation of all that we do every day.*

The Garden's Wall, choreography, Stephen Pier, 2012. *Photography by John Long*

4 | PROGRAMS, DEGREES, AND SERVICES

> 66 *Nothing can compare with the joy that can be derived from a beautiful performance, giving a good lesson or lecture, teaching a class, forming and directing new bands, orchestras, chamber music groups and opera companies, and opening the world of music to hundreds of human beings, old and young. It is my fervent wish, therefore, that this unique joy may be so great that you will give daily thanks to your Maker for being one of those whose lives are consecrated In the Service of the Beautiful.*
>
> Moshe Paranov, *Allegro Yearbook*,
> Hartt College of Music, 1952

In his 1949 JHMF Board of Trustees report, Moshe Paranov described the vibrant day-to-day activities at the school. He wrote, *"You would see here an administrative staff, teachers and students who express joy and love. You would see here the true meaning of fellowship. You would see here young men and women being guided by great masters of their craft. You would see here students practicing in every available inch of space including the coal bin and the washrooms. You would see here teachers and students hastening across the street to our overflow classes in the Hartford Public High School building. You would see here the human being in search of truth and everything which stands for true democracy."*

The celebrated reputation of the Hartt College of Music over the past century reflects a continuous dedication to high academic and performance standards, a belief in a comprehensive education, and the value of highly skilled professional artist-educators, and infectious collegiality. Integral to the school's success is its library, which serves as a resource and center for learning.

THE MILDRED P. ALLEN MEMORIAL LIBRARY

From its inception the founders and administrators of The Hartt School recognized the educational significance of a strong library. The Hartt Library was founded in 1938, at which time Gladys Pelletieri, wife of Hartt professor and director of the Julius Hartt School of Music (nonacademic division) Louis Pelletieri took care of a library collection. Funds were short. The faculty worked together communally, pooling resources and even growing some of their own food in a collective vegetable garden. The same common spirit prevailed during the creation of the library. The Pelletieris helped organize collections of books, scores, and recordings to build the library's

Ethyl Bacon, music librarian, 1960–1987, awarded Alumna of the Year by Dean Donald Harris.

collection. The Hartt Library occupied two rooms at 187 Broad Street.

After the library was moved to the University of Hartford campus with the Hartt School of Music in 1957, its name was changed to memorialize Mildred Pomeranz Allen (1908–1961). Allen was Connecticut secretary of state (1955–59), a pianist, music lover, friend of Hartt, and one of the university's founders. Allen received an honorary doctor of laws from the university in 1960. She also was vice president of the Symphony Society of Hartford and the Connecticut Opera Association. An Allen Memorial Fund committee, co-chaired by former governor John Lodge and Mrs. George Lane, raised over $40,000 to equip the new music library. More than 300 people attended the 1963 dedication ceremony, including Governor John Dempsey.

Allen Library dedication portrait of Mildred P. Allen by Furman Finck (based on photograph by John Haley), November 15, 1963.

Ethyl Bacon, library head from 1960 to 1987, provided valuable timelines and historical information about The Hartt School's history for future Hartt researchers.

In addition to her memorable affection for dogsled racing and making sweaters from her dog's fur, Ethyl's abiding humor and spirit were reflected in her colorful stories of the library's history:

> In 1946 Edward Broadhead became the head librarian. His assistant, Miss Wanda Schwerdtfeger, was famous for her efforts to control boisterous students with a promise of her homemade chocolate fudge. As a circulation librarian she remained for many years. Alumni do not remember the change from Dewey to LC, but they do remember Miss Wanda's fudge.
>
> About 1959 we were ordered out of the crowded music building. Everything was moved to the third floor in the north wing of Hartford Public High School, across the street. A highway detour at the time made crossing the busy street rather difficult. The last items to be moved were the performing collections, loaded into canvas laundry carts on wheels, pulled across, dodging traffic, then carried up the three double flights of stairs. Here it was extremely cold in winter and stifling hot in summer. And when the high school's marching band practiced beneath the open windows the noise was deafening.

In 1989, the library was moved again, though in more agreeable conditions than in 1959, from its location in

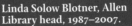

Linda Solow Blotner, Allen Library head, 1987–2007.

Tracey Rudnick, Allen Library head, 2009–present.

the Fuller Building to the Harry Jack Gray Center above Wilde Auditorium. Linda Solow Blotner was named library head and served from 1987 to 2007. She brought significant growth and initiatives to the library in her tenure as library head and remained active in the Music Library Association.

In May 2017 the Allen Library moved into a new facility located on the lower level of the Harrison Libraries Building (where the Mortensen Library is also located). The Allen Library became a "library within a library." Hartt students and faculty had vigorously affirmed their continued need for a dedicated library. The "New Allen" retained its specialized staff, amenities, and services, with most collections left intact. Tracey Rudnick, library head 2009–present, has worked tirelessly to lead many significant initiatives and to ensure that the new Allen Library will be a beautiful, functional, and first-class performing arts library.

In 1939 the library had about 9,000 items, and today has over 85,000, including more than 15,000 books and bound journals on music and dance; 40,000 musical scores; 20,000 sound recordings (including recordings of Hartt operas, concerts, and recitals); and 1,500 DVDs and videocassettes. Thousands of additional audio tracks are streamed online. Many dance items came from defunct institutions or organizations, including the Hartford College of Women's library, the Hartford Ballet's library, the Lila Acheson Wallace Library of the Juilliard School, and Dance Connecticut.

The library's mission has remained steadfast through its history. In partnership with faculty, the library is committed to the promotion of information and critical thinking skills that are essential to programs in the performing arts. To achieve these ends, the library fosters academic inquiry, scholarly communication, and lifelong learning by collecting, organizing, and disseminating information resources, and by providing instruction in their use.

The exterior of the Harrison and Allen Libraries, 2017.

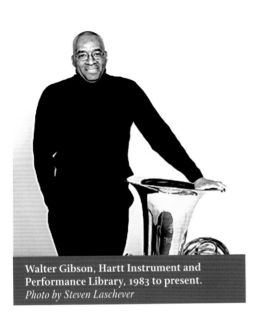

THE HARTT SCHOOL INSTRUMENT AND PERFORMANCE LIBRARY

In addition to the Allen Library, the school has maintained a library of scores and instruments. A Hartt trained tuba and euphonium player, Walter Gibson has overseen the Instrument and Performance Library operations for the Hartt School since 1983, providing thousands of scores and instruments to students and faculty over the years. The performance library, located on the second floor of the Fuller Building, was the original Mildred P. Allen Library. Today's recording studio was originally the office for the head librarian, a seminar room, and the collections. When the Allen Library was moved to the Harry Jack Gray Center, a shared connection was to be built between Fuller, the performance library, and the Allen Library, though this plan did not materialize. The service that Gibson and his student workers continue to provide is incalculable for the ongoing operations of the school. He remained a close friend to the Paranov family through the decades. And, based on his over 40 years of involvement with the school, Walter believes that its history can provide an enduring foundation for its future.

ACADEMIC STUDIES

Through the first several decades of its existence, instructors at The Hartt School, as in most schools of music, were identified by their instrumental or vocal performance specialty. The expectation, however, was that they would also teach other subjects. Sam Berkman, for example, taught courses in French, English, history, as well as the core music curriculum, including piano and harmony. Irene Kahn led and taught in the areas of opera, piano, and theory. Administrators often served dual roles as conductors and performers.

Consistent with Julius Hartt's belief that music students should have a well-rounded education taught by instructors with wide-ranging capabilities, Moshe Paranov wrote in his 1948 JHMF Board of Trustees report that a legitimate school should offer *"to the youngster, a thorough basic training; to the adult and layman, a program which leads to a deeper understanding and enjoyment of music; to the serious music student, a comprehensive course which will equip him to earn a livelihood in one of the many branches of this great art."*

In his 1949 JHMF board report Paranov compared reports from the 1940 catalogue on 222 Collins Street with the 1950 catalogue at 187 Broad Street. In 1940 only some of the musical instruments and a few theory classes were offered. In 1950 every musical instrument, including harp, was offered, and *"the history student could enter the field of musicology. The theory student would be prepared to teach all theoretical subjects in high school or college."*

MUSIC THEORY

Until the 1980s, music theory was taught within the scope of composition studies. For example, Tim Cheney was mentioned in 1946 as a "gifted young composer" and member of the theory staff who performed two of his compositions with the orchestra. At that time, theory and ear training were relatively new disciplines. Solfège, internationally taught to develop sight-reading skills, was offered in the Julius Hartt School of Music in 1920. In 1966 the faculty adopted a new curriculum for theoretical studies. The college written theory and ear-training courses previously offered in the first year were deferred to the second year. In their place intensive foundational work, developed by Tony Rauche, was

Dr. Patrick Miller, director of Academic Studies, 1983–present.

given in sight singing, dictation, and theory. By 1982, Dean Donald Harris had created an Academic Studies Department and identified three distinctive areas in the department: music history, music theory, and composition. He appointed Kerala Synder as director of academic studies and chair of music history, hired Patrick Miller to be the chair of theory, and James Sellars, chair of composition. Professors Imanuel Willheim and Myron Schwager served as chairs of music history after Snyder's departure for Eastman. Professor Nott became academic studies division director in 1995 and became chair of music history and B.A. music in 1997.

Since the 1980s, Patrick Miller's appointment as chair of music theory has created stability and distinction for the Department of Music Theory. Miller's research and resulting publications of Heinrich Schenker, culminating in a recording of Schenker's music, is significant for its impact in academia and for students' understanding of formal analysis and compositional principles. He was appointed director of academic studies in 1983. Through time, Miller, a National Teaching Fellow, skillfully managed the development of successful, sequential undergraduate, master's, and doctoral programs across the school, providing guidance and mentoring for faculty, staff, and administration. Most notably, Miller created the Hartt Music Theory Forum, bringing the greatest theoretical minds in the profession to the school to address students and faculty. In addition to his considerable responsibilities and accomplishments, he has composed and performed music for scores of silent films in the Hartford area, sharing this special art form with countless people.

Music History

Moshe Paranov invited the noted musicologist Alfred Einstein to join the Hartt faculty and teach courses in music history after leaving Nazi Germany in 1939. Einstein was internationally recognized for his extensive revision of the Mozart Köchel catalogue in 1936. In 1946 until his retirement in 1952, Dr. George Ross Wells chaired the Department of Academic Studies. In that year at its 187 Broad Street location, the enrollment of the College Department was 239, the nonacademic department, over 1,000, and 91 staff and faculty. Faculty who taught music history wore many hats, as did their predecessors in other areas. Imanuel Willheim was appointed chair of the history department, director of graduate studies, and director of the international studies programs in 1959. He expanded the history

Imanuel Willheim with Hartt faculty at the 2017 Hall of Fame Ceremony.
L–R: Robert Carl, chair of Composition; Kenneth Nott, chair of Music History; Michael Schiano, associate professor, Music Theory; Imanuel Willhelm, Joseph Mulready, Hartt alumnus, Julius Hartt Board of Trustees.

offerings during his tenure, and by 1977 reported that the department traditionally offered the History of Opera Survey, graduate seminars in bibliographic research, and the History of Musical Styles.

The Choral Collegium performed a great variety of rarely heard repertory from early music composers such as Purcell, Machaut, Josquin, Palestrina, and Bach. A Brass Collegium also performed on sackbuts and cornetti, which are still housed in the music library collection at the school. In 1977, Hartt College offered music courses in Afro-American music, Applied Music, Music Literature, and Music Theory to non-music majors as well.

Professor Myron Schwager was a member of the Hartt faculty from 1974 to 1993. Throughout his tenure at the school he served in various leadership positions: chairing departments of Theory, Composition, and Music History. Schwager is noted for his research on Julius Hartt and Ernest Bloch, as well as performing as a master cellist with the Karas Quartet for 30 years. The quartet was led by violinist Joza Karas, a member of the HSO for 50 years. Karas contributed a valuable history of music in Czechoslovakian Nazi concentration camps in his book, *Music in Terezín*.

Professor Kenneth Nott, a Hartt alumnus, was Schwager's graduate assistant. He studied with Willheim and was appointed chair of Music History in 1997. Nott won the prestigious Hartt Concerto Competition in 1977 and continues to make substantial contributions to music in churches and musical organizations throughout New England. Former Hartt students recall the remarkable experience in his history class when they observed and learned about his editing of Handel's *Jephtha* and then attended the performance by Hartt musicians, directed by Edward Bolkovac at Hartford's Trinity Church in 2014. One of Nott's fondest memories is playing the harpsichord continuo for the Hartt Chamber Orchestra performance in honor of Yehudi Menuhin at the Kennedy Center Awards in 1986. The experience exemplified Ken Nott's dedication to the Hartt School and perpetuating its high standards and reputation.

Professor Ken Nott (L) and student Michael Carlson in the Larsen Commons, Allen Library.

Today's Academic Studies Division

The music theory and music history faculty are collectively gifted and dedicated to their work as well. Dr. Michael Schiano, an accomplished pianist and accordionist, is recognized for his research and teaching of Mozart, Schoenberg, and the Beatles. His classes are sought after by Hartt students. Dr. Akane Mori, who studied with such noted academics as Allen Forte, David Lewin, and Claude Palisca is, a valuable contributor to the department.

Sight singing and ear training remain vital components of Hartt's music program. The multi-faceted Gabor Viragh, who supervises the ear-training program, received training in the Kodály Method in Budapest, Hungary, and studied with the top pedagogues of the Kodály movement. Viragh is also an accomplished jazz trumpeter and a faculty member in the Jackie McLean Institute of Jazz. Katalin Viragh brings extensive credentials as a violinist and member of the HSO as well as an artist teacher of ear training at Hartt. Alumna Donna Menhart, who has served in leadership positions for Kodály nationally, has been teaching ear training, music theory fundamentals, and harmony classes at Hartt since 1993. The distinguished artist teachers also include composer Kathryn Swanson, countertenor, conductor, and composer Benjamin Rauch, and Cameron Logan.

In music history, Professor Ira Braus is aptly recognized as a specialist in a wide range of musicological and theoretical subjects. In particular, his expertise in Brahms, Romantic and contemporary chamber music, and his scholarly pursuits in interdisciplinary research and cognitive musicology are time-honored by students and peers. As a medieval specialist, Dr. Charles Turner brought a wealth of knowledge of early music and co-directed the Hartt Collegium with violinist Emlyn Ngai and Ken Nott. Dr. Karen Cook now leads the studies in early music and is currently working on several new critical editions and translations of late medieval theory treatises as well as researching contemporary music. The department is strongly supported by Hartt composer and guitarist, alumnus Thomas Schuttenhelm and Jackie McLean fellow Krystal Klingenberg, who with an appointment as assistant professor of music history is the department's newest faculty member.

The Hartt Academic Studies Division has historically reflected the beliefs and values instilled by the school's founders, including a depth of strong, knowledgeable, talented teachers, and a dedication of the faculty to mentoring, not simply imparting information. The academic studies faculty emulates this synergy between scholarship and informed, competent performance ability.

COMPOSITION

With the belief that students would be "well-rounded" in their understanding of the art form, instruction in composition has been a constant staple in the curriculum at the the Julius Hartt School of Music since its inception. Hartt's Composition Department, now part of the Contemporary Studies Division, has a rich history of distinguished faculty composers who believe in performance-oriented pedagogy. Ernest Bloch, the preeminent Swiss-born composer, and Julius Hartt taught composition in the 1920–21 founding year of the school. In the early years students were also influenced by notable faculty composers including Isadore Freed, Nikolai Lopatnikoff, Arnold Franchetti, and Edward Diemente, who was a student of Freed.

Ed Diemente (L) and Stephen Gryc in the electronic music studio, 1985.

In 1948 Isadore Freed, chairman of the Composition Department, established the Institute of Contemporary American Music (ICAM) at Hartt. The American Composers Forum was established, in which six outstanding American composers provided important lectures to students and a concert of each of their works, followed by a discussion period. The composers in the first year included Frederick Jacobi of The Juilliard School; Otto Luening of Columbia University; William Schuman, president of Juilliard; Virgil Thomson, critic of the *New York Herald Tribune*; Walter Piston of Harvard University; and Isadore Freed. It was at this time that Frederick Jacobi composed an American opera, *The Prodigal Son*, which was premiered and dedicated to Moshe Paranov and the Julius Hartt Music Foundation. Jacobi was a visiting member of the Hartt School of Music faculty as well as head of composition at the Juilliard School.

Through the years, the ICAM brought in many of America's foremost living composers, including such luminaries as Aaron Copland, John Cage, John Corigliano, Chen Yi, Morton Feldman, Jennifer Higdon, Joan Tower, William Bolcom, and many more. ICAM presented concerts of their works for the general public and helped awaken audiences to the fact that American classical music is a living and vital art. Composers invited by the Institute regularly held open-form discussions with the student

Professor Ken Steen teaching Gala Flagello in the electronic music studio.

body, affording important opportunities for young musicians to acquire invaluable firsthand information and advice, based on sound practical experience, as to the techniques and problems of present-day composing.

In 1963 Edward Miller assembled Hartt's first electronic music studio in a vacant elevator shaft on the first floor of the Fuller Building. After Miller's departure, Edward Diemente became the second director of the studio as well as its most prolific user, composing many works on tape as well as works for electronic sounds with live instrument performance. Stephen Gryc, the third director of the electronic music studio, secured a New Music Resources Grant from the National Endowment for the Arts in 1985 to procure new equipment.

Both Gryc and subsequent co-director Robert Carl oversaw the transition from analog to computer-based synthesis. The current director of the studio, Ken Steen, has replaced the synthesizer-dominated studio with the most advanced digital audio workstation-based composition studio, complete with hardware and software available for synthesis, sound design, processing, editing, real-time performance, and the ability to realize works in a wide variety of forms in stereo through multi-channel formats up to 7.1 surround.

In 1965 the Rockefeller Foundation awarded the University of Hartford and the Hartford Symphony a joint $10,500 grant to enable them to give concerts of new symphonic works by university composers. Five of the Hartt College teacher-composers presented new works, including Arnold Franchetti, chairman of the Composition and Theory Department, Edward Miller, Edward Diemente, Alvin Epstein, and Thomas Putsché. The most unusual feature of the grant is the devotion of one program to new symphonic works written for children.

Composer Edward Diemente (L) and conductor Arthur Winograd share the score to *Pinocchio* with children for a 1965 ICAM program sponsored by the Rockefeller Foundation.

Famed Soviet composer-conductor Aram Khachaturian attended a student assembly in 1968 to hear three of his compositions performed by Hartt College students. Professor Vytautas Marijosius, chairman of the Applied Music Department, translated Khachaturian's comments, congratulations, and critiques of the performances.

Other full-time members of the Hartt School composition faculty that should be recognized include Timothy Cheney, Dean Donald Harris, Norman Dinerstein, Joseph Mulready, David Macbride, Larry Alan Smith, and Gilda Lyons.

Composer David Macbride at the keyboard

The current chair of Composition, Robert Carl, described the department's philosophy:

There are three core aspects to the current composition program's pedagogic philosophy, but they are deeply rooted in the nature of the school from its very outset. First, the creation of new music has never been seen as something "specialized" or "other" at Hartt. The writing of fresh works has been part of the school's ethos from its very start. Not only were distinguished composers a lively presence from the very beginning, but its founders had a hand in composition, including Moshe Paranov. The community continues to encourage the production and performance of new works by student, faculty, and guest composers on a regular basis, and assumes it to be part of a normal and necessary musical education.

Second, Hartt does not demand or promote a particular stylistic language for its composers at any level. While in earlier decades the range was inevitably narrower than it is today, Hartt has never been a "bastion" of any single practice. Not only have its composers continued to write in idioms ranging from traditionalist tonal to the most experimental, but the idea of diversity of expression is viewed as a key element to be preserved in its environment. And with the ever-increasing importance of technology to any composer's practice, students develop expertise with a wide range of devices and applications to enhance their vision. They also develop ongoing creative and professional relationships with the technologists who are majoring in the Music Production and Technology program.

Hartt composition faculty and friends celebrate after a rousing Foot in the Door concert at Arizona State University, 2019.

Third, collaboration has been a fundamental element encouraged throughout the program. In its current form, the school has active joint projects between Composition and the Dance and Theater Divisions, as well as film and video score composition. In addition, within music itself, the program has created continuing annual collaborations with the orchestra, wind ensemble, Performance 20/20, Foot in the Door, visiting chamber ensembles, and individual instrumental and vocal studios. And the student composers are given opportunities to collaborate amongst themselves, with the biannual Public Works Concert Series and the Composers' Ensemble. In short, the key to Hartt's relation to new music is that it is seen as a natural element of music making, one that is key to a young musician's growth and success.

DANCE

Dance instruction began at the Julius Hartt School of Music between 1934 and 1935. Hartt's modern dance curriculum was based on collegiate dance programs developed by Hanya Holm at Colorado College and Bennington College. Alwin Nikolais (born in Southington, Connecticut, and a student of Truda Kaschmann) implemented this curriculum as the primary teacher for the adult (or college) dance program until he left to join the army, serving from 1942 to 1946. Ms. Kaschmann ran the program in his absence and beyond and was one of the most influential modern dance teachers in the greater Hartford region. In addition to the adult dance programs at Hartt College, a children's dance division was developed to offer both ballet and modern curriculums in the late 1940s.

Enid Lynn (L) teaching, School of the Hartford Ballet, Hartford, Connecticut, circa 1970.
University of Hartford Archives and Special Collections

In 1948, Moshe Paranov wrote to Nikolais to convince him to return to Hartford to build a dance department.

> 66 *Before I depart for that locale known as heaven (where I shall be head of a very important musical school with the finest Dance Department!), I am first going to have a dance department at the Julius Hartt School of Music. When that time comes, you [Nikolais] will be an integral part of this activity.*

Nicholais was a significant contributor to the development of dance at The Hartt School. As Hartt's first modern dance instructor, he choreographed dances for his students and several operas. His association with the American modern dance community helped Hartt engage numerous modern dance pioneers for master classes. After leaving Hartt, Nikolais became one of the most highly decorated artists of the twentieth century. Among his many awards were the National Medal of the Arts and the Kennedy Center Honors in 1987.

Throughout the 1950s and 1960s the children's dance program, directed by Truda Kaschmann and Dorothy Silverherz, became autonomous and separate from the Hartt College. Adult dance classes continued to be a part of the Hartt Opera Department curriculum, and by the 1970s and 1980s, faculty from the School of the Hartford Ballet were employed to teach dance at Hartt.

Truda Kashmann and Alwin Nikolais, Hartford, circa 1939.
Courtesy of the Wadsworth Atheneum Archives

Truda Kaschmann with young students, Hartford, circa 1950.
University of Hartford Archives and Special Collections

Development of Ballet Pedagogy and Dance Performance Degrees

Hartt College's association with the Hartford Ballet continued in 1971. Under the artistic direction of Enid Lynn, the Hartford Ballet collaborated with Hartt by performing *The Nutcracker* and other repertory works under the baton of Moshe Paranov. Meanwhile, Enid Lynn continued to develop a post-secondary ballet teacher's training program at the School of the Hartford Ballet, called the Teacher's Training Certification, with the hope to join forces with the Hartt School in creating a ballet pedagogy degree program.

At an eventful meeting at a Moe's restaurant in Hartford, Dean Larry Alan Smith, Community Division director Michael Yaffe, and Enid Lynn began planning for a bachelor's degree program in dance in association with the University of Hartford. A certification was the foundation for the present-day BFA in dance, ballet pedagogy emphasis/major. The new Dance Division began with Enid Lynn as director of the School of the Hartford Ballet and BFA Dance Division administrator and founder. Former soloist with the Martha Graham Dance Company Peggy Lyman Hayes was hired as the first dance division director. The BFA dance program accepted its first freshman class in 1994, graduating them in 1998.

After the bankruptcy of the Hartford Ballet in 1998 and then Dance Connecticut in 2000, the University of

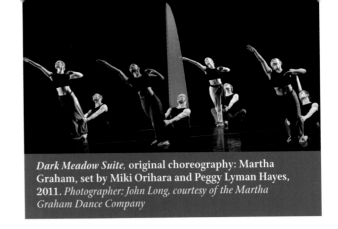

Dark Meadow Suite, original choreography: Martha Graham, set by Miki Orihara and Peggy Lyman Hayes, 2011. *Photographer: John Long, courtesy of the Martha Graham Dance Company*

Hartford and The Hartt School took ownership of the ballet company's assets, which included sets, costumes, sewing machines, costume shop furnishings, and even an antique fuel pump. Some things were sold, while others are still used by The Hartt School. After the BFA program began in 1994, the School of the Hartford Ballet and then the School of Dance Connecticut continued until the University of Hartford and The Hartt School absorbed the dance school into the Hartt Community Division in 2004.

In the first few years of Hartt's collegiate dance division, the program grew slowly, with five to eight students in each incoming class. Amy Lesko Manfredi, present administrator of the Hartt School Dance Division and in the first graduating class of 1998, recalls the unique partnership between the Hartford Ballet and Hartt Dance. This collaborative relationship allowed a select group of Hartt students an opportunity to perform with the Hartford Ballet during their college years.

(L–R) *La Sylphide*, original choreography: August Bournonville, restaged by Hilda Morales, 2011; *Petruschka*, choreography, Stephen Pier with original choreography by Michel Fokine, 2013; *Carmen*, choreography: Debra Collings Ryder, 2014. *Photographer: John Long*

In October of 2009, Hartt's Dean Aaron Flagg asked Stephen Pier, who was teaching at Juilliard to help in leading the dance division. In February of 2010 Pier became the full-time director believing that the division *"needed momentum and direction. It had good bones, a serious program that needed a professional world mindset."*

Stephen Pier, supported by his exemplary faculty, is taking significant steps in advancing the quality and recognition of the dance program. Professor Katie Stevinson-Nollet, Hilda Morales, Ralph Perkins, Debra Collins Ryder, and Nina Watt, together with the division's other outstanding dance teachers, foster a collaborative environment, mentoring, and high standards so that students will develop a value system that prepares them for diverse career paths and professional mindsets.

Collaborations with Hartt composition faculty and students as well as Hartt ensembles are a regular part of the curriculum. Lief Ellis, Hartt manager of Performing Arts Technology, collaborated on projects with Nina Watt and Katie Stevinson-Nollet. A monumental production of *Petruschka* was performed in 2013. The jazz division collaborated on *Ellington Dances,* and the guitar department collaborated in a performance of *Carmen.*

INSTRUMENTAL STUDIES

Many Hartt School alumni heard Moshe Paranov reflect on a life cycle of a musician.

> ❝ *At 20 they know everything. At 30 they still feel they know a little something. At 40 they'll start to wonder, at 50 they're not sure, at 60 they get frightened, at 70 they ask any musician they know how to understand a certain piece, at 80 they get hysterical, at 90 when they don't know nothin,' they know somethin'. If you love music, learn music, devote your life to it.*
>
> Moshe Paranov,
> *Video-Hartt: 165 Years of Music,* 1990

A comprehensive review of instrumental studies at The Hartt School would be extensive and beyond the scope of this book. Most certainly, notable names will go missing in this brief summary, but hopefully future researchers will study and document the many talented performers and teachers who have graced our school over the past one hundred years. Through the decades the tradition of inviting world-famous performers to enhance the full-time faculty in the academic and community divisions continues.

This section will be divided into instrument families and some specialty areas.

BRASS

In the 1970s the New York Brass Quintet was in residence at Hartt College. At that time the ensemble was the only quintet of its type to concertize throughout the world, presenting music from all periods. All of the players taught at Hartt College, including Robert Nagel, trumpet; Allan Dean, trumpet; Paul Ingraham, French horn; John Swallow, trombone; and Thompson Hanks, tuba.

In 2009, students studying trumpet at the Hartt School celebrated Roger Murtha's 45 years of teaching and service to the University of Hartford, the longest tenure of any faculty member at that time. Murtha's influence was ubiquitous at the school and in the Community Division. He received three degrees from the Julius Hartt School of Music and performed with the Hartford Symphony Orchestra for 47 years. Today his students perform and teach all over the world.

President Walter Harrison (L) presents Roger Murtha, joined by his wife, Janis, a plaque in honor of his 45 years of teaching at the Hartt School.

Recognized bass trombonist John Rojak brought valuable pedagogy and repertoire to Hartt. Ronald Borror taught and mentored many outstanding trombone players through his years at Hartt, including alumnus Matthew Russo. Gilbert Johnson studied at the Hartt College from 1945 to 1949. Johnson was principal trumpet for the Philadelphia Orchestra and is heard on many of their great recordings from the Ormandy era. Armando Ghittalia was a Hartt faculty member and principal trumpet for the BSO for 28 years. He edited and published the Hummel trumpet concerto (now a staple of the trumpet repertoire) and was the first to record it.

Today innovative and acclaimed trumpeter Phil Snedecor leads the department. Virtuoso trombonist Haim Avitsur joined the Hartt faculty in 2016 and brings his versatile expertise to the department as well. They are joined by highly credentialed senior artists including James Jackson III, principal euphonium player for the US Coast Guard Band and conductor of the Hartt Symphony Band; David Wakefield, horn player for the American Brass Quintet; Scott Mendoker, recognized tuba soloist and teacher; and Barbara Hill, principal horn player for the Hartford Symphony Orchestra since 2006. John Rojak, Ronald Borror, David Wakefield, and Kevin Cobb, who succeeded Roger Murtha, were members of the American Brass Quintet. Notable faculty included Chris Gekker, Ray Mace, Greg Whitaker, and Jay Lichtmann. The brass faculty at Hartt has through time continued to represent the high performance reputations expected and honored at the school.

EARLY MUSIC

Lutenist Joseph Iadone directed the Hartt Collegium Music in the 1960s. The programs of early music varied in genres and historical styles but generally included music from the medieval to baroque periods. Iadone understood that audiences would have to listen differently to early music repertoire. In a 1971 interview, he claimed,

66 *They've got to learn to hear. People had a much greater awareness of sound a few hundred years ago. They knew how to appreciate the tune and its parts. There is too much sound today; the instruments get louder and louder, they blast at us and we move further back, making no effort to listen. But there is still some hope, and I have all the faith in the world that the student who likes early music will lead us back to listening.*

Edward Clark, Hartt College of Music organist and harpsichordist, echoed Iadone's sentiments and to this day regularly performs with early music ensembles. Today the Hartt Collegium is led by Professor Kenneth Nott and acclaimed historical and modern violinist Emlyn Ngai.

Guitar and Harp

Dick Provost founded the guitar department after graduating from Hartt College in 1960. When he began his studies at Hartt he played jazz guitar and worked with Joe Iadone in early music performance. While he was studying piano in graduate school with Irene Kahn, she recognized early on that he was more interested in guitar than piano. Irene convinced Dean Sam Berkman to allow Provost to go to New York to study classical guitar. Subsequently, he began teaching and founded the guitar department in 1968, which provided instruction for countless noted performers. Provost studied composition with Arnold Franchetti and believes that in-depth study of the academic side of music is necessary for high-quality teaching and performing. Provost regularly brought in world-famous guitarists such as Oscar Ghilia, Manuel Barrueco, Jason Vieaux, and the Los Angeles Guitar Quartet for residencies and master classes. His expectations reflect the commitment to high standards of musicianship for Hartt faculty, both collegiate and noncollegiate.

(L–R) Peter Clemente, Dave McLellan, Chris Ladd, Leo Brouwer, and Dick Provost celebrate Brouwer's eightieth birthday at Hartt, March 2019.

Christopher Ladd and Peter Clemente were former students of Provost's. Ladd chairs the guitar studios today, and Clemente offers an eclectic approach to the guitar studio. Together they continue to promote the excellent musicianship and teaching techniques of their teacher, Dick Provost. Hartt alumnus and artist teacher Susan Knapp Thomas leads an active harp studio and serves as a chamber music coach.

Keyboards

In the stories related to the founders and friends of The Hartt School, piano performance has been a staple of the school's curriculum in the academic and community divisions. Organ performance was also historically highly prized at The Hartt School.

In 1945, Moshe Paranov hired Ray Hanson to teach piano at the Julius Hartt School of Music. Hanson studied with Harold Bauer and taught at Hartt for more than 40 years. He chaired the department until his retirement in 1992 and performed with major orchestras around the country. In 1973, Hanson married pianist Anne Koscielny, an internationally acclaimed pianist whom European critics called "a major American pianist." Distinguished pianist and teachers Paul Rutman and Louis de Maura Castro furthered the exceptional talent of the piano faculty. Both continue to teach today. Much beloved Watson Morrison concertized often in New England and was known as an interpreter of Bach.

Rose Mende, who served in administrative capacities with The Hartt Community Division, taught and mentored Margreet (Maggie) Francis, who co-chairs the piano department today. Maggie regularly performs with the Hartford Symphony Orchestra and is actively involved in The Community Division.

Since receiving his DMA from The Hartt School, David Westfall has conducted many international and national tours and residencies, and actively performs in chamber groups. Westfall served as the co-chair of the keyboard department and division head of the Instrumental Studies Department. The piano faculty traditionally teaches in the school and Community Division. Hartt students from all programs study applied piano with alumnus Gregory Babal. Since he started teaching in 1983 Greg has reached over 3,000 students.

John Holtz, chair of the Hartt organ and liturgical music faculty, Elizabeth Sollenberger, and Edward E. Clark, members of the faculty, presented organ concerts that marked the first professional use of the new Gress-Miles Organ, an instrument of three keyboards and pedal board, 37 ranks, and 2,192 pipes, which was a gift to Hartt from Alfred C. Fuller. The three performed a series of virtuosic contemporary organ music beginning in June of 1971.

The Gress-Miles Organ pipes, 1971.

PERCUSSION

Alexander Lepak, a member of the Percussive Arts Society Hall of Fame, was a professor at the Hartt School of Music at the University of Hartford from 1950 to 1991. He was the author of the *Friese-Lepak Timpani Method* and many other books that have become standard texts worldwide. His *Concerto for Mallet Instruments* has been performed in the United States, Canada, and throughout Europe. He was also solo timpanist and principal percussionist with the Hartford Symphony. Ben Toth, Lepak's successor as head of the percussion studio, remarked that *"Lepak founded the percussion program at The Hartt School in 1950, making it one of the first in the country. All of the accomplishments of the Hartt Percussion Department since that time are reflective of his influence."* Lepak's influence resonates with the culture of the school as Toth promotes and advances his enduring legacy.

In 1992, when Toth was hired as department head, he also introduced world music to the Hartt percussion curriculum, including percussion music from Africa, Cuba, Brazil, the middle East, Caribbean steel pan ensembles, and jazz vibraphone. The classes are taught by outstanding artist teachers who specialize in world music genres, including John Amira (Cuban percussion), Rogerio Boccato (Brazilian percussion), Joe Galeota (African percussion), Ted Piltzecker (jazz

(L–R) Hartt percussion chairs Al Lepak and Ben Toth

vibraphone), and Shane Shanahan (Middle Eastern percussion). Professor Toth directs the Hartt Steelband. Percussion students today receive a comprehensive and professionally stringent program of studies.

STRINGS

The history of exceptional string students and faculty at the Hartt School is impressive. Hartt College of Music graduate in music history and contrabassist Bertram Turetzky named lutenist Joseph Iadone and oboist-scholar Josef Marx as his two most important influences. Turetzky saw the emergence of the contrabass from a traditional position in the orchestra to an important and versatile solo instrument. Hundreds of new works were written for and performed by Mr. Turetzky, and he is remembered as the father of modern bass playing.

Contrabassist Gary Karr taught public school music in Hartford early in his career as well as lessons at The Hartt School. Karr is recognized as one of the most riveting performers of the instrument who raised the standards of playing as well as expanded the repertoire to include contemporary solo and ensemble literature. In 1961 Olga Koussevitzky gave her husband's contrabass to Karr.

Karr's career took off in 1962 when he performed with the New York Philharmonic Young People's Concerts directed by Leonard Bernstein. Karr taught today's double bass Hartt faculty member and department chair Robert Black. Black graduated from Hartt College in 1979, served as an adjunct professor beginning in1993 and full time professor in 2003. He brings memorable energy and excitement to his performances of contemporary music on the contrabass, and frequently collaborates with artists from diverse disciplines in his performances.

Mrs. Serge Koussevitzky presents a gift of her husband's 1791 contrabass to Gary Karr, double bass player and Hartt faculty member.

True to Hartt tradition, the school's string faculty were and continue to be nationally and internationally recognized performers and teachers. Famed cellist Raya Garbousova taught at Hartt College. Violinist Renato Bonacini was a highly recognized associate professor of violin and ensembles at Hartt and regularly performed with Hartt ensembles. He was the assistant conductor and concertmaster of the HSO until 1970. Grammy nominee Elmar Oliveira studied at Hartt College with Ariana Bronne and Raphael Bronstein.

The full-time string faculty now are led by award-winning and internationally active artists Anton Miller (violin) and Rita Porfiris (viola), and Mihai Tetel (cello). Senior artist teachers Terry King (cello) and Steve Larson, Melinda Daetsch (viola), as well as principal artist violin teacher Katie Landsdale augment the exceptional talent and experience of the studios. Violinist Emlyn Ngai is nationally and internationally recognized for his gifted baroque violin interpretations as well as modern performances. Together, the string faculty at Hartt perpetuates the tradition of highly skilled, actively performing musicians.

Katie Stevinson-Nolette and Robert Black rehearse *Je ne sais quois,* **2018.** *Photographer: Jeff Teitler*

CHAMBER ENSEMBLES

In the 1950s The Hartt String Quartet performed professionally as well as taught at Hartt College. Bela Urban and Martin Katahn, violinists, and Robert Ridolfi, violist, and Kermit Moore, cellist, were string faculty members who were instrumental in developing chamber music study at the school. Today the Hartt String Quartet continues to perform with current string faculty members.

From 1980 to 2001 The Hartt School was privileged to have the Emerson String Quartet in residence. The Emerson, named after American essayist and poet Ralph Waldo Emerson, is recognized as one of the most prestigious and active string quartets in the world. They were the first chamber ensemble ever to win the Grammy Award for Best Classical Album and Best Chamber Music Performance as well as *Gramaphone* magazine's Record of the Year award. The Emerson brought international recognition to the Hartt School through their illustrious reputation. They taught private lessons, coached, and conducted an annual competition with students playing with the quartet. Though the early years of their long tenure with Hartt was a bit shaky, Humphrey Tonkin, when becoming university president in 1989, regarded the group as "one of the crown jewels" of the university. He awarded them a Distinguished Service Medal in 1994. Alumna Barbara David was among a group of faithful concert subscribers and supporters who called themselves "The Transcendentalists." This group raised enough funds to make the quartet's services affordable and kept them a viable member of the university community that brought recognition and strong students to Hartt.

Following the Emerson's departure in 2001, the Miami String Quartet served as Hartt's quartet-in-residence from 2003 to 2009. In addition to the Miller-Porfiris and Adaskin Trios and the long-standing residency of the Lion's Gate Trio, the Richard P. Garmany Series, led by founding curator Steve Metcalf, currently brings four highly touted chamber ensembles to campus each year for performances and residencies.

Woodwinds

Woodwind instructors and performers were an important part of the Hartt family from the start. The student orchestras and bands were infused with professionals to assure high-quality performances as well as a way of providing valuable mentoring for future musicians. Alan Francis, a Hartt graduate, recalled that after Rose Mende retired, Donald Mattran continued to accelerate the practice of bringing in highly recognized performers to enhance instruction and performance at the school. In true Hartt tradition, Alan Francis conducts Community Division ensembles as well as teaches clarinet students for The Hartt School.

Clarinetist Curt Blood joined The Hartt School collegiate faculty in 2006 and teaches for the Community Division as well. Award winning clarinetist Ayako Oshima serves

as a valued member of the faculty, along with senior artist Yousun Chung. Other notable senior woodwind artists include oboist Kemp Jernigan and bassoonist Marc Goldberg. Janet Arms leads the collegiate flute studio, and Greig Shearer, the principal flutist with the Hartford Symphony Orchestra since 1993, actively teaches in the collegiate and community divisions. They were preceded by distinguished flautist John Wion, professor of flute and chamber music at Hartt from 1977 to 2007.

With his forward-thinking vision, Moshe Paranov attempted to hire Sigurd Rascher to teach saxophone in 1940, but due to work visa issues had to rescind the offer. Internationally recognized saxophonist Stanley Aronson was a full-time woodwinds teacher at Hartt College from 1959 to 1984. Aronson, a member of the Glenn Miller band and the Hartford Symphony, was equally skilled in flute, clarinet, and his primary instrument saxophone, and recognized for purity of tone.

Donald Sinta, a classical saxophonist, educator, and administrator, served on the Hartt faculty from 1967 to 1974 and performed regularly in Hartt College concerts. Sinta was instrumental in the development of the American saxophone sound and the creation of the American school of saxophone playing. Specializing in contemporary music, he is known for his technical abilities as well as his distinctive and personalized musical interpretations. He is highly regarded for his incorporation of string playing and vocal traditions into the expressive vocabulary of contemporary saxophone playing. As with many Hartt faculty, Sinta wore many hats. He taught his primary instrument and a woodwinds class for music education students. Additionally he directed the Concert Band, the Pops Concert, the Hartt Summer Music Program, and the Contemporary Music Festival for a year. He left to replace his teacher Larry Teal at the University of Michigan upon Teal's retirement. Following Sinta's tenure, Phil DeLibero, James Hill, Lynn Klock, Ken Radnofsky, and Michael Menapace taught saxophone. The saxophone studio is now led by Carrie Koffman, a student of Sinta's. Since she began in 2003, Koffman has advanced Sinta's work through new commissions, an extensive performing career, and a strong commitment to students.

Large Ensembles

Large instrumental performance ensembles have been an integral part of The Hartt School since its inception. Moshe Paranov directed orchestras and choirs for decades. Lithuanian conductor Vytautas Marijosius joined the faculty of the Hartt College of Music in 1950. For nearly 35 years he served in many roles: teaching opera, serving as chair of the Department of Applied Music, and director of orchestral activities. Marijosius also conducted HSO concerts. The American Prize–Vytautas Marijosius Memorial Award in Orchestral Programming is now given in his memory.

Through the decades, many highly respected conductors led the Hartt Orchestra among their other teaching and conducting responsibilities. In 1999 Christopher Zimmerman was appointed Fuller Professor of Orchestral Studies at Hartt. He directed the Hartt Symphony Orchestra, and was the Music Director of the Hartt Symphony. Today Dr. Edward Cumming is the Primrose Fuller Professor of Orchestra Activities for Hartt following his tenure as the Music Director of the Hartford Symphony Orchestra. His depth of experience and expertise brings exceptional professionalism to instrumental studies at Hartt.

The ensembles perform a wide variety of genres and repertoire and have maintained the highest standards for pre-professional performances that

Vytautas Marijosius conducts the Hartt College of Music Orchestra for the 1971 Concerto Contest winner, Peter Woodard, performing Ravel's *Piano Concerto in G.*

are the hallmark of the school. Professor Glen Adsit serves as the director of bands and conducts the Wind Ensemble as well as the celebrated Foot in the Door new music ensemble, created by Hartt composer James Sellars. Hired in 2000, Adsit was the first person hired exclusively to direct bands. As he approaches his twentieth year, many milestones have been accomplished, including major performances at the College Band Directors National Association for nine of those years. His bands have performed over forty individual and consortium commissions and have produced four Naxos recordings.

Together, Adsit and Cumming generate a tour de force in instrumental ensemble program quality. Students of conducting receive expert guidance and mentoring and have gone on to lead major musical organizations. With traditional and contemporary programming, celebrated

Edward Cumming, Primrose Fuller Professor of Orchestral Activities (L), and Glen Adsit, director of Hartt Bands and Foot in the Door Ensemble, teaching conducting lessons.

guest artists, and unique collaborations, Hartt students experience unrivaled ensemble music making.

JAZZ

On November 4, 1942, MacDowell Award winner Stanley Freedman opened Hartt's Faculty Series with a set consisting of different styles of jazz, including swing and boogie-woogie. Moshe Paranov wrote, *"This is in the nature of an experiment and is the first step toward the inauguration of a department of popular music in the school. He plays this kind of music with great skill and it is my suggestion that you come and spend an evening listening."*

The Jazz Department was formally inaugurated in January of 1943. Stanley Freedman, however, left for the service on January 27, 1943, so Paranov vowed to build up the department after the war was over.

JACKIE McLEAN

66 *He has played jazz with the majesty of a Greek god, and today remains one of the few surviving icons from a golden era of jazz that will probably never be equaled.*
Jazz Educators Journal, 1998

Jackie McLean, saxophonist and composer, began his distinguished career while growing up in New York's Sugar Hill neighborhood in Harlem, where notable artists, writers, and musicians such as Duke Ellington lived during the late 1940s. The musical environment was electric and innovative. Harlem was filled with clubs, including the Apollo Theater, that featured some of the world's most notable jazz musicians. At age 15 McLean met legendary pianist Bud Powell who also worked with Thelonious Monk, Sonny Rollins, Charlie Parker, Miles Davis, Lester Young, Charles Mingus, and Art Blakey. Bud Powell mentored the young McLean and later received encouragement and mentoring from Charlie Parker (Bird), the renowned alto saxophonist. Powell invited Jackie into his home and shaped his musical and personal growth. For two years Powell coached and mentored McLean, and then Miles Davis gave him his first break by inviting him into his band after only four years of playing. From Davis and Mingus, McLean learned style concepts that later influenced his teaching throughout his life.

As a member of Art Blakey's Jazz Messengers, McLean described drummer Art Blakey as

 the greatest of all the band leaders I ever worked for. He was a big brother/father figure. Art allowed the guys in the band to be creative, to write music and perform it in their particular fashion. He also had an open door for young talent and he wasn't afraid to take an unfinished musician and put him in the band and polish him up and finish him off and make him a real performer. I loved Art very much and I loved the time that I played with him.

René McLean (L) and his father, Jackie, performing for students, 1988. *Photo by Maurice D. Robertson*

McLean carried these experiences with him, and they became the foundation of his philosophy in developing the future African American Music department at the Hartt School of Music, and the Artists Collective, Inc.

In the late 1950s and 1960s he was living on New York's Lower East Side, working in clubs where he was instrumental in developing the renowned Slugs Saloon as a jazz club. He also performed and recorded, primarily for Blue Note, and taught. His son René was his first student, a saxophonist and multi-reed instrumentalist who is a world renowned musician and educator in his own right.

The civil strife of the '60s had a profound effect on McLean's sense of style and harmony. He reflected,

> **❝** *A musician is always aware of his environment. He reacts to the world around him. When John F. Kennedy was shot, I knew it would have an effect on music. All of those assassinations within a 10-year period—Medgar Evers, Martin Luther King, Malcolm X—along with the civil rights movement, were reflected in the music.*
>
> *New York Times*, April 25, 1990

It was at this time in 1967 that Jackie met Phil Bowler, a bassist, and other Hartt students who came to his performance at the popular New York City jazz club Slug's Saloon. They invited him to come to the Hartt College of Music to teach a class and to meet Moshe Paranov, the college's president. In 1968, with Moshe's support, McLean began commuting from New York City to present lectures on the history of so-called "jazz music" and its origins from slavery to the bebop era and international connections. He also served as a consultant for the Connecticut Commission on the Arts under Executive Director Anthony Keller during the Ella Grasso administration. In 1970 Jackie and his wife Dollie and daughter Melonaé moved to Hartford, later followed by son Vernone. Jackie began teaching African-American music history at Hartt full time. That year he and Dollie also founded the Artists Collective, a non-profit community-based arts education organization in Hartford's North End. From its beginnings the Artists Collective has created a safe haven for youth by offering intense training in the arts with emphasis on cultural awareness and social skills. Thousands of youth, the majority of whom are of African American, Caribbean, and Latino descent, have been given an opportunity to express themselves in a safe, positive setting while growing into caring, responsible adults. Many have become educators, doctors, and professionals in other fields.

By 1982 Dean Donald Harris formally approved the African American Music Department and a new undergraduate program, Jazz Studies. McLean was named chair. Dizzy Gillespie received an honorary doctorate from the Hartt School that year as well. From the students' perspective, the intersection of "high art" or classical tradition with jazz as the music of the people, and contemporary music that crossed tonal and formal musical boundaries, created a learning environment second to none. Saxophonist Sue Terry was the first person to earn a BMUS in Jazz Studies (African American Music) in 1981. Jaki Byard began teaching repertory building, piano, and arranging in the mid-1970s continuing until 1987.

Al Lepak was a key proponent of Jazz Studies and conducted the Concert Jazz Ensemble at Hartt until 1991. As a graduate of the African American Music Department, Steve Davis succeeded Lepak as conductor of the jazz ensemble, which was renamed Hartt Big Band. Chris Casey conducted the group beginning in 2000.

Nat Reeves performing, 1988. *Photo by Maurice D. Robertson*

In the same year, Jackie's department of African American Music was officially renamed the Jackie McLean Institute of Jazz, or JMI. The department continues today to build on the foundation of personal relationships and cultivating young talent. Faculty in the department are actively performing musicians who, through their own music making, mentor their students.

Bassist Nat Reeves, though not a Hartt alum, was mentored by McLean and became a member of his band. Reeves is most notably recognized as a premier musician and educator. He was honored by the University of Hartford for his scholarly and artistic creativity in May 2015. As a prominent resident of the City of Hartford, the mayor proclaimed June 22, 2013, as Nat Reeves Day in honor of "his music legacy and contributions through the world."

Peter Woodard, who was tapped by McLean to become chair of the Jazz Department in 1994, recalled, *"Jackie populated his faculty with people he personally mentored. Jackie was a one-man effort to bring African-American culture into the center of the university culture"* (Shanley, *Jazz Times*, 2008–9, p. 38).

McLean could identify the strengths and energy in his students and guide them to their future work. Steve Davis, who began studying with McLean in 1985 and graduated from Hartt in 1989, recalls that Jackie was an inspiration who "gave a lot of himself for future generations" (Shanley, *JazzTimes*, 2008–9, p. 38). Jazz pianist Larry Willis was discovered and recruited by Jackie on the Blue Note release *Right Now!* The jazz faculty today perpetuates Jackie's spirit and legacy as they pass on his values, beliefs, and musicality, and René McLean continues teaching the history of the development of African American music.

Among his numerous national and international awards during his lifetime, Jackie McLean received the Jack Lang (French Minister of Culture) Medal *Officier de l 'ordre des arts et des lettres* during France's bicentennial celebration at the time of the Mitterrand administration in 1989, and the National Endowment for the Arts Jazz Master Award in 2001.

A year after his death in 2006 Jackie was inducted into the DownBeat Hall of Fame. The next year the University of Hartford posthumously awarded McLean an

(L–R) Larry Willis, Nat Reeves, Steve Davis and students in class at Hartt. *Photo by Maurice D. Robertson*

honorary doctorate of music degree and Dollie McLean a University of Hartford honorary doctorate of fine arts. In 2017, Dollie and daughter Melonaé accepted a Hall of Fame Award from the Julius Hartt Foundation Board of Trustees, led by James Barry and Marcos Carreros, in honor of Jackie's contributions to The Hartt School and the university.

During Peter Woodard's leadership as chair of the department he maintained and built on the reputation of the Jackie McLean Institute (JMI). He was encouraged by his students to invite jazz vocalist Shawnn Monteiro to present a master class. With no vocal jazz program offered at the time, Woodard recognized the tremendous value that Monteiro's internationally acclaimed teaching and performance skills would add to the program. In 2006 Monteiro joined the Hartt jazz faculty. Today each vocal jazz student receives a private lesson, two repertoire classes, and two classes in performing with a band as part of their program.

In 2013 jazz saxophonist Javon Jackson was named the director of jazz studies at The Hartt School. In 2018 Jackson created a master's degree in jazz, promoting future growth of the department. His dedication to further the traditions of the Jackie McLean Institute has maintained the special quality of the department by bringing in the most prestigious jazz artists to work with Hartt students. In a 2018 *DownBeat* article he said,

> 66 *Knowing Jackie as I did and the kind of person he was and his commitment to starting that jazz department, it's been an honor to follow in his footsteps. I want to help the next generation of musicians as much as I can.*
> Kassel, *DownBeat*, January 2019, p. 19

Jackie's role as a mentor of young talent is in clear evidence by the fact that a good portion of the present-day JMI faculty are graduates of the JMI Jazz Studies Program. Many of these notable alumni have established international careers as exceptional performers and educators.

Dollie (L) and Melonaé McLean (R) and Hartt trustee Marcos Carreras, 2017 Hartt Hall of Fame Awards.

MUSIC EDUCATION
New Degrees and Accreditation

On July 20, 1940, the Julius Hartt School of Music became the first independent institution in the state granted the right by the Connecticut State Department of Education (CSDE) to confer the bachelor of music degree. Music education courses were approved by the CSDE in 1942. Summer sessions were popular with teachers as well as undergraduate students. The classes were taught by the school's full-time faculty. In 1948 the JHSM became the first independent music school in Connecticut to be granted approval to award the master of music degree. Rose Lischner, temporary officer of the first JHMF Board of Trustees in 1934, was appointed supervisor of all instrumental music in Hartford.

Hartt's relationship with the Hartford schools, as with much of the Hartford community and surrounding public and private schools, continues to this day. Elmer Hintz, then director of music in the Hartford Schools and head of the Music Education Department at JHSM, worked to grow the department, and several students graduated who were actively teaching in Connecticut. The growing pains of the school caused the faculty in the academic and nonacademic areas to coordinate their resources, as Moshe described in his October 1946 board of trustees report, "perfect teamwork." In 1948 with the leadership of Sam Berkman, the board of trustees announced that the Hartt College of Music had received accreditation and election to the National Association of Schools of Music as an associate member. The school was voted a full member of NASM in 1950. The bachelor of music education and master of music education degree programs were approved by the Connecticut State Department of Education in 1951. By 1956 Elmer Hintz reported a 400 percent growth in enrollment in the Music Education Department of Hartt College of Music. In 1945–46, 18 students had enrolled in the program. By 1955–56, 79 students enrolled, including 10 graduate students. Rose Mende was named assistant chairman of the department with responsibilities for overseeing student teaching.

Rose Lischner teaching a music education class

A task force report in January of 1964 reiterated the beliefs and values of the school's founders. Changes were made in the music education curriculum to more closely align with the university's school of education and the requirement of the accrediting body, NCATE.

However, the task force warned that "*the Hartt Music Education program is an outgrowth of and emerged from a strong professional program in music. Its object was to develop professional musicians who would be able to transmit their enthusiasm, high professional standards, skills and concepts of excellence to the young people in public and private schools.*" Furthermore, the task force suggested that a sixth-year program for music educators and a major in music therapy be created and a doctoral program "doctor of musical arts" be initiated.

By 1966 the university conferred 20 bachelor of music education degrees and 7 master of music education degrees. Hartt College was ranked in the top 10 of music schools in the country.

The Music Education Department continued to grow, led by Donald Mattran, who joined the faculty in 1966. Mattran served as chair of the Department of Music Education, director of the summer session, and director of the Summer Youth Music Program, which he founded in 1968. The doctor of musical arts in music education, composition, and applied music was granted in 1976. During his tenure as dean from 1971 to 1980, a new financial support program and the curriculum expanded.

In 1978 Bill Willett became chair of the Music Education Department for the Hartt College of Music. In his annual report he cited his department's many

accomplishments, including his own appointment as president of the National Association of College Wind and Percussion Instructors. In his 1978 chair's report to the school's director Donald Mattran, Bill Willett described the impressive growth of the music education program.

 In 1977 Susan Engle and Alexander Farkas were appointed as teachers of the general education and Kodály methodology and ear training programs at the school. Dr. Wayne Dvorak created a course, Evaluation in Music Education, to meet the need for documented justification of music in schools. Electronic piano labs were integral to the curriculum and essential for growing technology in schools. Music education students also learned teaching techniques for recorders and guitar in the classroom at this time. Undergraduate students who wished to continue their pursuit of licensure in music education were assessed in their competencies in sight singing, keyboard harmony through Sophomore Evaluations.

Evaluation in Music Education was taught at that time by Dr. Wayne Dvorak, and Electronic Piano Lab was taught by Barbara Smith and Janet Eckhart, and for many years to the present by Greg Babal. Sophomore Evaluations were instituted in 1977–1978, which helped to ensure strong musical competencies for music education students.

In the summer of 1980, Kodály summer courses were moved to The Hartt School from Watertown, Massachusetts. To this day, the Kodály methodology has continued to serve as the foundation of music education at the Hartt School. Levels I and II of Orff and Dalcroze training have also been offered over time.

Music Education faculty often assumed leadership roles in the Hartt School. Manny Alvarez chaired the Music Education Department prior to becoming associate dean and interim dean in 1989. Douglas Jackson, percussionist and music education conducting instructor, assumed the role of associate dean. Clark Saunders, who served as director of graduate studies in music education, associate dean and interim dean of the Hartt School, and currently associate provost for the university, established the guidelines that today provide high standards and expectations for all doctoral candidates at the school. A PhD in music education led by Saunders was approved in 1994. Professor Dee Hansen assumed the roles of director of graduate studies in music education, director of Hartt Summerterm, and director of graduate studies for The Hartt School.

Many significant music educators have contributed to the strong reputation of the department through the decades. Kathleen Goodrich started the String Project at the University of Hartford Magnet School. Other string faculty included Richard Rusack, Nola Campbell, and Joshua Russell, who followed John Feierabend as chair. The vocal/choral music education faculty included James Jordan (chair 1986–1990), and Drs. Al Holcomb, Geoffrey Reynolds, Stuart Younse, Vanessa Bond, and Julie Hagen. A significant author and educator specializing in improvisation and creativity, Dr. Chris Azzara led instrumental studies in music education. He was followed by Dr. Kim Reese and Dr. Warren Haston, who served as program chair for undergraduate studies and is currently director of Hartt Summerterm.

Succeeding acclaimed choral director and educator James Jordon as chair of music education, Dr. John Feierabend brought a strong emphasis in his First Steps and Conversational Solfège Kodály program. His wife Lillie taught elementary music at the University of Hartford Magnet School, where she provided an impeccable model of brilliant musicianship and pedagogy. John and Lillie together were instrumental in envisioning and designing the University of Hartford Magnet School's Multiple Intelligences theme and educating thousands of future music educators. Their contributions to a "tuneful, beatful, artful learning community" have created an enduring foundation for training music educators nationally and internationally.

John and Lillie Feierabend teaching Hartt Summerterm classes

Summer Sessions

Collegiate and noncollegiate summer sessions began in 1943. In 1948 supervisors from East Hartford, Manchester, New Haven, Bristol, and other towns worked toward their master of music degree and approximately 40 other college students continued work on their undergraduate degrees. By 1949 the summer sessions ran for six weeks, at which time academic classes as well as clinics for voice, string, and band methods were offered.

The Hartt School Summerterm graduate music education program continued to grow and expand its services with nearly 400 annual course registrations for music educators in America and Internationally.

Summerterm at Hartt

VOCAL STUDIES
OPERA

In 1933, four years before his retirement, Julius Hartt, sensing the national interest in opera, encouraged the school to begin an opera program. In October of 1942, the Julius Hartt Musical Foundation Board of Trustees announced the inauguration of the opera department. An article in the *Hartford Times* commented, *"The Julius Hartt School in its new opera department follows its own tradition of setting its standard at the top. It is difficult to progress upward from the top but this amazing institution judged upon its record can be expected even to manage that."*

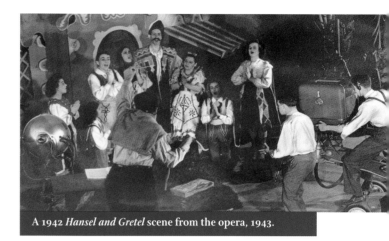

A 1942 *Hansel and Gretel* scene from the opera, 1943.

In the fall of 1942, Elemer Nagy, noted Yale University director of drama and scene designer for Yale Music Association operas, was appointed head of the Drama Department of the Julius Hartt Musical Foundation. The first Hartt opera production, a double bill, featured Franz von Suppé's *Ten Maidens and No Man*, and the first Hartford performance of Paul Hindemith's *Here and There*, with Hindemith conducting.

Hansel and Gretel was the first grand opera event to be completely prepared and presented by any music school or local group. In 1943 Hartt presented *Hansel and Gretel* as the first complete opera on television by General Electric TV station WRGB in Schenectady, New York, directed by Moshe Paranov. Friedrich Schorr coached the singing and staging, and Dr. Nagy oversaw the acting, costumes, scenery, and lighting. In addition, Dr. Nagy and Moshe Paranov led a class in operatic training. The class and the collaboration of Nagy, Paranov, and Irene Kahn pioneered work in developing an American opera culture at Hartt.

The Hartt College of Music Opera Department presented hundreds of operas through the years, including *The Marriage of Figaro* and *Don Giovanni* for the first time in Hartford. The policy of singing opera exclusively in English was implemented to attract American audiences. These full-length operas were never excerpts or scenes and were staged and styled according to the highest professional standards. At that time, all of the costumes and sets were designed by Elemer Nagy, and all of the costumes were made under Pauline Paranov's supervision.

In her memoirs of Hartt history, Ethel Bacon, the Hartt College librarian, recalled *"Music-making nearly twenty-four hours a day! Building opera scenery in the sub-basement 'til 3 a.m.!"*

Dr. Elemer Nagy, collaborating with Boris Goldovsky at Tanglewood, received wide acclaim for his successful experiments in developing plastic operatic scenery, light in weight and easy to dismantle. In a further phase of his experiments, Dr. Nagy devised a multi-projection system using Corrulux, twin projectors and slides, to create scenic moods.

At that time it was thought that the success of these experiments could well revolutionize the operatic picture. The mobility of the sets made it possible to take opera to many communities that otherwise would not be able to afford building the wood and canvas sets in use at the time. In 1968 Chancellor Archibald M. Woodruff presented Elemer Nagy with a Quarter Century Club Award from the University of Hartford for his twenty-five years of service.

Nagy scene panel projections and scene from early opera

Through much of its early history the Hartt Opera Guild, founded in 1945, helped fund the opera productions. The guild's membership skyrocketed from 200 to 450 in 1946. The Julius Hartt School of Music orchestra provided music for all opera performance and was composed entirely of its 70 students. The Guild's subscribers from the greater Hartford community each paid a membership fee in the mid-1950s of seven dollars. Only 50 cents of this fee was used to purchase season tickets to the opera productions. The chief functions of the Guild were to promote interest in Hartt opera and to assist in securing paying audiences without extensive advertising costs.

In the 1960s, opera students attended master classes by international stars. Some of these singers joined the Hartt faculty, including William Diard, internationally proclaimed tenor who was also featured in the title role of Hartt Opera-Theater's first production, *The Tales of Hoffmann*, in the spring of 1968. Diard joined the faculty in the fall of 1967. Arthur Thompson, a 1964 graduate of Hartt College of Music, performed in the opera as well. Elemer Nagy provided the stage direction and design, including his now-famous multi-screen scenery projection system. Hartt operas were always performed in English.

Jennie Tourel, famed opera and concert star, continued her series of master classes in 1968, and soprano Esther Hinds presented a benefit concert to raise money to purchase stage equipment for the Millard Auditorium.

In 1973 Jack Zei was called to Hartford and asked to head the opera program at the Hartt School of Music at the University of Hartford. He became the chair of the Hartt Opera and artistic director of the Hartt Opera Music Theater and started a summer musical

theater that always packed the house. In 1978 he was promoted to professor of opera. Together with his wife Joyce, a brilliant vocal coach and teacher, they created a well-respected and celebrated opera program. Jack was also coordinator for the *comprimario* roles and chorus for Connecticut Opera and brought outstanding master teachers to Hartt College, including Charles Nelson Reilly and Robert Lawrence. Celebrated soprano, stage director, and teacher Addie Bishop succeeded Jack Zei as artistic director of the opera theater from 1982 to 1993.

The opera program at Hartt declined for the next few years due to financial and technical issues. In 1999 tenor Wayne Rivera was appointed to reinvent the program. It was at this time that musical theater was emerging as a viable program at the school. But Wayne believed that "teaching people the fundamental techniques of singing is the same regardless of genre or style." The academic year 2000 highlighted the Hartt Opera Theater concert version of Copland's *The Tender Land*. Wayne created an abridged version of the work and then contacted librettist Erik John (the nom de plume of Horace Everett) to write original dialogue. The resulting world premiere of the production was performed in the Asylum Hill Congregational Church with Gary Miller, then senior minister at the church narrating, and Hartt's Edward Bolkovac conducting.

Opera at The Hartt School continues under the capable directorship of Doris Kosloff. Kosloff succeeded Edward Bolkovac as division director of the Vocal Studies Department. Doris greatly expanded live streaming for the Mainstage opera productions and directed and conducted many successful performances, including Kurt Weill's *Street Scene.*

(L -R) Wayne Rivera, Erik John, and Edward Bolkovac celebrate the world premiere of the adaptation of Copland's *The Tender Land.*

CHORAL

In 1966 Dr. Gerald Mack was appointed the head of choral activities. He became one of the most recognized leading choral directors in the U.S. at this time. For 27 years his groups performed along with Hartt's band and orchestras at most National Music Educators conventions. He established a master's degree in choral conducting. Dr. Mack also directed the Greater Hartford Youth Chorale and the Worcester Choral Society. Robert Christensen became the director of the Greater Hartford Community Chorus in 1976. Gerald Mack's successors included Rick Coffee, Pam Perry, and Paul Oakley. These choral directors helped sustain the choral tradition at The Hartt School and provide the vocal forces needed to perform large-scale instrumental and choral works.

In the 1970s Alexander Farkas taught the Kodály techniques at the school. An interest in this methodology began to be adopted in the U.S. as a way to foster music literacy for all students. A few years later, Paul Oakley was preparing *Carmina Burana* for a performance, and Edward Bolkovac was being considered for a choral conducting position in music education. When Bolkovac was given a few moments at the podium, he immediately demonstrated his ability to conduct the choir and at the same time effectively lead the orchestra.

Performance of the Verdi *Requiem* in St. Joseph's Cathedral, Hartford, 2012.
Photo by Bob Mulllen, the Catholic Photographer

was honored as the OAKE National Chorus twice and performed for the annual conferences in Springfield and Hartford. Collaborative performances with the New Haven Chorale, the Hartford Chorale, and the Hartford Symphony Orchestra included the Brahms *Requiem*, included in the New Haven Subscription Series, and Verdi's *Requiem* in the Cathedral of Saint Joseph. Performances also included travel abroad, with one of the more memorable trips to Hungary.

Edward Bolkovac (second row, left) and the Hartt Chamber Choir overlooking the Danube in Budapest, Hungary.

John Feierabend also knew of Bolkovac's work and asked him to apply for the position. In 1999, when Oakley became ill, Malcolm Morrison appointed Ed Bolkovac as head of the Choral Department.

Bolkovac brought to The Hartt School a systematic, professional approach to choral singing which honored historically recognized performance practices. Though many exceptional performances have taken place over the decades, several stand out. The Hartt Choir

Voice

Hartt full-time voice faculty included celebrated mezzo-soprano Janine Hawley from 1996 to 2001, Jerry Pruitt, Fritz Moses, and Johanna Levy. Celebrated alumni studied at Hartt during this time. Noted bass-baritone Ryan Speedo Green was a voice student of Joanna Levy and studied Opera Workshop with Wayne Rivera. Green received his bachelor of music degree at Hartt and was a Metropolitan Opera National Council Audition award winner. He held lead roles in *Trial by Jury*, by Gilbert and Sullivan, *The Old Maid and the Thief*, by Menotti, and Offenbach's *Orpheus in the Underworld*.

Javier Colon, a music education major at Hartt and voice student of Wayne Rivera, is best known as the winner of *The Voice* on NBC in 2011. Lin-Manuel Miranda, creator of *Hamilton,* studied voice with Rivera at Wesleyan University. Interestingly, Miranda elected to study classical music at the college so that he would have the technical capabilities of singing many styles of music.

Dionne Warwick attended Hartt College of Music in the 1950s. She was honored for her distinguished career when she was named Alumna of the Year in 1971. In 1986, President Stephen Joel Trachtenberg, on behalf of the University of Hartford, awarded her an honorary degree by the university for her life accomplishments. The tradition of singing remains strong and vibrant at the school with a notable, gifted voice faculty including

Dionne Warwick, seated next to Jackie McLean, receives an honorary degree in 1986.

Robert Barefield, Cherie Caluda, Deborah Lifton, and many other outstanding artist teachers, including Hartt alums Michelle Fiertek and Benjamin Rauch, and Wayne Rivera, Claude Corbell, Kelly Horsted, Sondra Kelly, Maureen O'Flynn, Kyle Swann, Eric Trudel, and Chai-Lun Yueh. In true Hartt tradition, collaborations among divisions and colleagues are common.

Soprano Cherie Caluda and Hartt Symphonic Orchestra conductor Edward Cumming celebrate the 2017 performance of Larry Alan Smith's *Epistulae ex Ponto.*

THE 1980s

Before his departure in 1980, Donald Mattran proposed some organizational changes, which were approved by the executive committee of the board of trustees on May 23, 1979:

1. A change of name for the academic division to the Hartt School of Music.

2. A change of name for the present nonacademic Hartt School of Music to Non-credit Division of the Hartt School of Music.

3. A change of name for the head of the institution to dean rather than director.

The cover of program celebrating Moshe Paranov's 95th birthday and the 70th birthday of the Hartt School

In 1980, Donald Mattran left his position as dean of the Hartt College to take a sabbatical and the return to full-time teaching and conducting. Donald Harris was appointed dean by Stephen Joel Trachtenberg, the University of Hartford president. Donald Harris had been chair of the Department of Composition and Theory, director of the Institute of Contemporary American Music (ICAM), and a composer-in-residence at the Hartt School since 1977, coming to the Hartt College of Music from several administrative roles at the New England Conservatory. Harris was known as a deeply devoted advocate of the arts. In an address in 1988, he wrote,

> *Our mission as artists and artist-educators is above all humanitarian. We are the true guardians of the nation's spiritual life. We understand instinctively that no civilization can ever be remembered fondly or commemoratively if its artistic contribution is negligible. The arts are a fundamental part of the humanizing process.*

Harris served as dean of the Hartt School of Music for nine years. He later assumed the position of dean of the College of the Arts at Ohio State University. Manny Alvarez, who had been Hartt's associate dean for academic affairs since 1983, and Stuart Schar, dean of the Hartford Art School, served as acting deans between 1988 and 1990.

A caricature of Moshe Paranov by Al Hirschfeld

5 | A NEW CENTURY, A PERFORMING ARTS INSTITUTION (1990–2020)

> " *The message of the artist is about human experience, no matter how sorrowful or joyous, it has the potential to be ecstatic. You will carry with you the dark rumbles of Sophocles' voice, or the exquisite majesty of Bach's music or the painful sensual eloquence of Martha Graham's soaring imagination. They are works of art that infect our imagination and excite our own need to make a statement. Remember that Art is not only the music we play, the dance we dance, the play we act, it is the summation of our experience. Art is living and living is an art.*
>
> Malcolm Morrison, 2008

THE 1990S: PREPARING FOR THE NEW CENTURY

In 1990 the 70th anniversary of The Hartt School and Moshe Paranov's 95th birthday were celebrated with many events and performances. A caricature of Moshe Paranov by Al Hirschfeld was unveiled in New York. One hundred and sixty-five prints were each sold for $1,000 to benefit the Moshe Paranov Chair at the Hartt School. The original print was presented to Paranov on May 16, 1991, at the gala benefit concert in Lincoln Theater.

The Hartt 165 Years of Music celebration featured the Hartford Ballet, directed by Michael Uthoff, Grant Johannesen, pianist; the Portland String Quartet; the Hartford Symphony Orchestra; Michael Lankester, conducting the Connecticut Opera Association with George Osborne, general director, Robert Ashens, resident conductor, and Arthur Thompson, baritone from the Metropolitan Opera, with the Hartt Commencement Orchestra, Stanley DeRusha, conductor.

Moshe Paranov and Dean Larry Alan Smith celebrating Paranov's 95th birthday and the 70th birthday of The Hartt School.

The 1990s brought significant changes to the Hartt School of Music. Larry Alan Smith was appointed dean in 1990. Early in the decade the university and the region suffered from a serious, unforeseen downturn in enrollment and financial challenges. Dean Smith reluctantly made cutbacks to programs, faculty, and staff to deal with the situation. At the same time he imagined that the school could grow in dramatically different directions. In 1991, he presented a list of ideas that represented a rethinking of nearly every aspect of the school.

Among them:

- The addition of dance, theater, and stage technology
- The creation of a pre-professional program for grades 11 and 12 or 9–12 in music, theater, and music theater
- The creation of a music technology center
- Construction of a performing arts center
- Renovation of the existing Hartt facilities
- Expansion of international exchanges involving faculty, staff, and students
- Development of an arts magnet elementary school and day-care center on campus for the purpose of performance, education, and research
- A change of name to The Hartt School (in 1993)

The ideas were then documented in a 27-page long-range plan. In the mid-1990s, Smith, formerly dean of the School of Music at the North Carolina School of the Arts, contacted Malcolm Morrison, who had been dean there from 1976 to 1987, for advice on developing Hartt's theater curriculum. Morrison asked,

 Are we this music school we talk of from the past, or are we a performing arts school that moves into the future?

By 1994 the results were demonstrable. Joseph Mulready, chairman of the Hartt Board of Trustees, reflected,

"Four years ago, when Larry got here, the Hartt School's annual deficit, as reckoned by the university, was running about $1.3 or $1.4 million annually. This year, for the first time in anybody's memory, we're going to have a balanced budget, or close to it. Many people who have been around here a long time were convinced that such a turnaround was impossible. Larry made it happen." (Steve Metcalf, *Hartford Courant,* Sunday, May 8, 1994)

Dean Smith's vision for the school's future identity, his directives to increase enrollment, and an energetic focus on fund-raising paid off. Attention to community partnerships also expanded, including a comprehensive cooperative agreement with the Hartford Symphony Orchestra signed in 1993. Larry Alan Smith stepped down from his role as dean in 1997. In 2000 he returned to teach composition at The Hartt School until his reappointment as dean in 2018. All of the initiatives Smith envisioned have come to fruition, and new plans are on the horizon for the school.

A 21st-Century Performing Arts School

Walter Harrison, who was named president of the University of Hartford in 1998, recognized the extraordinary vision of Dean Smith and sought a worthy successor to his accomplishments. At Smith's invitation, Malcolm Morrison joined the Hartt theater faculty as its first director in 1996.

His wife, Johanna Morrison, a consummately talented actor and teacher in her own right, became a valued member of the Hartt theater faculty at that time and remains so today.

With Larry Alan Smith's departure, Malcolm Morrison was tapped as interim dean in 1997 and served as dean of The Hartt School from 1998 to 2008. Morrison was a beloved, impassioned, eloquent orator whose wisdom and humor are fondly remembered today. His words expressed his strong belief in the value of the arts and in many ways reflected the writings of Julius Hartt and Moshe Paranov. From his commencement speech, May 16, 2004:

66 *The artist has the extraordinary privilege of making ideas and speculation tangible. Or as that great sage Erma Bombeck said, "It takes a lot of courage to show your dreams to someone else." Indeed it does. It is the raw exposure of intimate and deeply personal experiences, which embody a hugely sensitive area of our intellect, emotions and experiences. On the other hand, that is what the artist is about, making private thoughts public, so that the most sensitive areas of human experience are palatable and through art we extend our experience of them.*

Many of the theater initiatives that were proposed and activated under Larry Alan Smith's tenure were turned into reality by Malcolm Morrison. Dean Smith's efforts to secure funding for the school's growth and expansion resulted in an $18.6 million bequest from Primrose Fuller. This gift, like the many other generous contributions from the Fullers, allowed the school to invest in Hartt's students and facility. The Mort and Irma Handel Performing Arts Center (HPAC) opened its doors to theater and dance students in 2008.

Morrison fought a long-term battle with cancer and passed away on Friday, November 8, 2013. In his final convocation address to students in 2008 he said,

" *As many of you know I shall be stepping down as Dean at the end of this year—the real year—on December 31st. You are the inheritors and representatives of a distinguished legacy and so I say to you and to all who have gone before you, "thank you." Thank you for the opportunity to serve this school. It has been an exhilarating adventure that reaffirms my unalloyed conviction that we as human beings have infinite possibility and that with good will we can conquer the negative things around us and… at the very best… give joy and hope to many. I wish you all an exhalted place in the history of this school and in your careers. Again…"thank you."*

Johanna and Malcolm Morrison celebrate the opening of the Mort and Irma Handel Performing Arts Center; first day of classes with students and faculty at the HPAC.

President Harrison wrote in a message to the university community upon Malcolm Morrison's death,

> 66 *Malcolm cared lovingly for the School, and poured his energy into nurturing talent and providing opportunity. He attended student and faculty performances of all sorts almost every evening. I marveled at his energy and real enjoyment of so many genres of art.*

Malcom Morrison's successor as dean, Aaron Flagg, who began in 2009, worked to strengthen relations with the Julius Hartt Board of Trustees and alumni. He also hired Javon Jackson to assume leadership of the Jazz Department and to form a partnership with the Stamford Symphony. In 2013 a plan to renovate Millard Auditorium, coined "Fuller at 50," was initiated by Steve Metcalf and supported by Dean Flagg. Generous donors, including Robert and Frankie Goldfarb, propelled the Millard restoration project. A grant from the Richard P. Garmany Fund at the Hartford Foundation for Public Giving launched the Richard P. Garmany Chamber Music Series, which brought in world-class performers to The Hartt School.

CONTEMPORARY STUDIES

Moshe Paranov may have been envious of the title "Contemporary Studies," which embraces a wide vision for future opportunities in performing arts education. He understood the need for including contemporary music, jazz studies, dance, and theater in addition to classical music study. He also understood that it was important to have audio and video documentation of performances and guest artist services. However, to encompass an entire division of The Hartt School as a place for ever-expanding studies and degree programs that could provide employment for students was a concept that needed a twenty-first-century vision.

Led by Hartt alumnus and composer Professor Ken Steen, the division's programming is diverse and flexible in response to current needs of the performing arts world. Still, the pervasive thread that permeates all programs at The Hartt School is the belief in high standards for artist training. Degrees in contemporary studies include stringent academic and performance entrance expectations and coursework. Students who elect to major or minor in a contemporary studies area learn to be performing artists, arts administrators, excellent composers, recording engineers, and music industry professionals.

The construct of Contemporary Studies includes the time-honored Composition Department, whose history we reviewed in chapter 4. Additionally, the Music Industry Department involves several programs, including Music Production and Technology, Music Management, and Performing Arts Management.

MUSIC INDUSTRY

THE BEGINNINGS

When Nina Paranov was in high school, Bela Urban, chair of the Strings Department at Hartt College, gave her a tape recorder, with which she immediately began recording operas and concerts. Her work is regarded as fundamental to the establishment of the recording programs at Hartt. In 1948 Moshe Paranov announced that classes would be offered in the technique of recording and the science of acoustics in relation to recording and broadcasting. Nina became the audio director for the Hartt School of Music in 1961. She worked with Hartt librarian Ethyl Bacon for eight years in an effort to preserve the recordings. Though the standard method for preservation would have been categorized by the Library of Congress, Nina created a cataloguing system for archiving tapes of the performances that could include multiple nights of the same performance. Thanks to her organizational skills and care of these early recordings, efforts to preserve and archive concerts, master classes, and recitals are under way today.

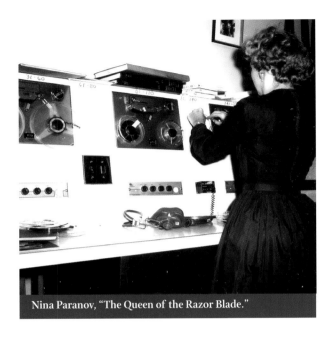

Nina Paranov, "The Queen of the Razor Blade."

In 1978, composer Ed Diementi invited David Budries to work with Nina to expand and develop the recording studios. On his first day on the job, Nina, whom David described as "the most quiet backbone of the institution," sheepishly explained that most of the recording equipment did not work. Together they rebuilt the recording studio. At this time there were no schools to teach how to record and preserve recordings, and it was not clear that the recording arts could be a viable degree program. But David and Nina worked together with the early recording technology, and by the late 1980s his proposals to create a Music Production and Technology (MPT) program were instituted.

Music Production and Technology

Hartt's music production and technology degree was modeled after the European Tonmeister program, training musicians to become sound engineers. With this approach, students would be better prepared to make artistic decisions for high-quality recordings, such as determining the type of microphones needed for different genres and instrumentation. Not surprisingly, Jackie McLean required jazz students to take recording classes so that they could work more effectively with recording engineers.

When Budries was named the head of Sound Design at the Yale School of Drama in 1999, Scott Metcalfe, a Hartt composition graduate, stepped into the important role of overseeing the recording initiatives at The Hartt School. He had been mentored by David Budries and taught the sound technology classes for him. Scott now leads the program at the Peabody Conservatory, which began in 1983.

In 2003 Nina Fagan passed the torch to a new recording studio coordinator, Kathleen Zavada-Machose, a graduate of the Hartt MPT program. Kathleen expanded the role by solidifying the service activities of the studio as an important educational component for the students in the MPT degree program. In 2012 Matt Baltrucki, a graduate of the prestigious graduate program in sound recording at McGill University,

took over the position and was hired as an adjunct faculty member in the MPT department. Today Koby Nelson, a Hartt MPT alumnus, is the recording studio coordinator and, with Gabe Herman, leads the efforts to preserve Hartt's historical recordings. Nelson also serves as an artist teacher along with Jim Chapdelaine, a West Hartford–based award-winning musician and recording engineer.

Philosophically, the program mirrored what has been historically valued at The Hartt School. The students were training to not just be technicians, but to be musicians as well. In 2009, Justin Kurtz assumed the role of chair of Music Production and Technology at Hartt. Under his leadership the program continued in the tradition of educating students in all aspects of musicianship, from theory to performance, along with courses in electronics, acoustics, and technical training in the recording studio. Supported by Dean Betsy Cooper, funding was secured to renovate and construct a new recording studio within the Fuller Music Building in 2017.

In the summer of 2018 faculty member Gabe Herman designed and oversaw construction of the new studios to ensure they would be of exceptional quality and functionality. In addition to serving as assistant director of the MPT program since 2009, Herman also served as interim chair of the Music and Performing Arts Management between the years 2016 and 2018. Herman was appointed assistant professor of music industry in 2018 and currently teaches courses in both the MPT and Music and Performing Arts Management Departments.

Music and Performing Arts Management

The Music Management (MUM) and Performing Arts Management (PAM) programs at The Hartt School reflect a carefully thought out relationship between art and business that prepares students to enter a wide variety of fields in the commercial and not-for-profit avenues of the entertainment industry. Both of these degrees offer a skills-based curriculum with project-based courses, hands-on-experience inside the classroom, and a required internship that provides practical experience within an organization. As an important component of the Music Industry program, both the Music Management and Performing Arts Management programs continue to play a significant role in preparing music students to enter a wide variety of fields.

The bachelor of music in music management provides both instrumental performance training and specialized instruction in arts management. As an example, David Budries cited the Emerson String Quartet, and in particular cellist David Finkle, as providing a valuable model for music management during their years of residency at Hartt. The bachelor of arts in performing arts management provides similar specialized curriculum in arts management, with an expanded selection of courses in business and a concentration of electives in communications or business instead of instrument study. In addition, these students graduate with a defacto minor in business administration.

Harmon Greenblatt initially taught the Music Management courses and was the first chair of the department. Irene Conley expanded the program offerings and served as the chair of the Music and Performing Arts Management Department as well as the Hartt School director of undergraduate studies. Conley's leadership embraced the philosophy of preparing artists to deal with the business matters of their profession, and for arts management students without a performance degree to help professionally trained artists deal with the business of their profession.

In 2018 Marcus Thomas, an accomplished educator and entertainment attorney, became chair of the Music Industry Department. Thomas brings experiences from major record labels, music publishers, and music print publishing. Mehmet Dede, an experienced music producer and arts consultant with an internationally recognized profile, joined the department in 2016 as a teacher and mentor to future music industry leaders. The leadership and faculty in the Music Industry Department offers business, legal, and technology production expertise. Students have many opportunities for internships and field trips to important cultural centers such as Boston, New Jersey, New York, and Nashville in order to gain a practical perspective and a lifeline to the field. In Hartford students have worked with Real Artways, Infinity Hall, Telefunke, the University of St. Joseph, and Cheney Hall in Manchester.

The full-time and adjunct faculty of this department maintain professionally active careers in the industry and bring real-life industry knowledge to their courses and mentorship. This new chapter of the music industry program has received renewed support from the school and university and promises to thrive well into the future.

Theatre

The history of theatre at The Hartt School began with the opera program in the 1940s. Elemer Nagy's development of the multi-projection system and the focus on opera-theatre productions at the school and in traveling ensembles represented the priorities for music-theatre productions at that time. Nagy served as chair of the Opera Department well into the 1960s. Nagy brought with him from the Yale Drama Workshop the methods of the "little theatre," based on the principle "that the playwright, actor, and stage technician inspire one another by learning each other's jobs." The Hartt College Opera Department then applied that principle in the collaborations of the composer, stage designer, director, conductor, orchestral musicians, singers, dancers, and state technician. The successful fusion of music and stage-craft had far-reaching repercussions when the future department of theatre was developed decades later.

Nagy's influence significantly influenced Hartt students. Kent McCray, a famously celebrated production manager and producer in the television industry, recounted in his 2017 book of memoirs the many memorable experiences and lessons learned in his time at Hartt. In 1947 he planned *to shadow and work for a highly-accomplished theater expert/musician who was about to give me a very comprehensive, well-rounded education.* (McCray, p. 18)

In 1951 a proposal for an educational lyric theatre project was presented to the Ford Foundation for a grant to help fund an all-purpose theater that would seat 600–750 people. It included a 50-foot proscenium and an orchestra pit, as well as a television stage for direct broadcast of live productions. The proposal also called for a theater-in-the-round and a recital hall.

In 1963 Isaac Stern gave the inaugural performance in Millard Auditorium, the primary performance venue in the Fuller Music Building. The desire to erect a versatile theatre complex became a reality decades later when the Handel Performing Arts Center was built and the Theatre Division was created. Nagy remained the stage director and designer of what came to be known as Hartt Opera-Theatre, until 1969, two years prior to his death.

Theatre productions such as plays existed on the university campus primarily through Hillyer College and its literature department. David Watson, whom Alan Rust later brought to the Hartt drama faculty, taught courses at Hillyer as part of an arts and sciences program for non-majors, essentially a liberal arts school drama program with different goals than a professional theatre training program.

Larry Alan Smith, Malcolm Morrison, and Alan Rust had forged close professional alliances prior to coming to Hartt. They joined Smith when he was appointed dean, and in the mid-'90s worked with Michael Yaffe,

associate dean of the Hartt School, to establish an acting degree. With their guidance the theatre degree was approved, and auditions opened for the program in 1995. In the fall of 1996 the first class of theatre students began. When Dean Smith stepped down in 1997, Malcolm Morrison became the interim dean, and Alan Rust became the director of the division of theatre. Classes were held in Gengras. Berkman Auditorium was turned into a black box (which was later turned back into a performance venue). There were 14 students the first year, two of whom were later nominated for and one who won a Tony Award. In the second year more space was needed. It was at that time that theatre was taught in various locations at the Hartford College for Women until Handel Performing Arts Center was built.

In the 1980s music theatre was part of vocal studies, but Malcolm Morrison moved it into the theatre program with BFA degrees in actor training and music theatre. Some of the first productions were *Brigadoon* and *Much Ado About Nothing*.

Once on This Island, 2007, directed by Ralph Perkins. Photographer: Larry Rowe

HARTT THEATRE

TODAY AND BEYOND

Though it is the youngest division at The Hartt School, theatre is the most competitive degree program, with more applications than any other division. Alan Rust initiated professional partnerships with significant theatre entities including the Hartford Stage Company, Goodspeed Musicals, Monomoy Theatre, and TheatreWorks. Students are able to experience a comprehensive training through degrees in music theatre and actor training. Faculty members of the Theatre Division are eminently qualified and experienced. Their credentials range through all walks of stage life, nationally and internationally. Full-time faculty including Robert Davis, Diana Moller-Marino, Tracey Moore, Ralph Perkins, Alan Rust, and David

Watson are supported by outstanding artist teachers and senior artist teachers, including Annmarie Davis, Robert Felstein, Kristin Huffman, Tracey Marble, Johanna Morrison, Carolyn Paulus, John Pike, Mark Planner, Larry Raiken, Janelle Robinson, Joni Weisfeld, Mark Womack, and Debbie Markowitz (production stage manager). In 2011 the school mourned the loss of associate professor of theatre Kevin Gray, who brought high standards to Hartt's professional theatre training.

Based partially on the number of graduates in Broadway plays, the school was recognized as a premier school to look for talent by *Playbill* magazine in 2018. A highly successful program in London, England, also offers students the opportunity to study abroad, with unique training and performance opportunities.

The Life and Adventures of Nicholas Nickelby, 2016, directed by Alan Rust, Robert Hannon Davis, and Annmarie Davis. Photographer: Larry Rowe

INTO THE FUTURE

This historical account of The Hartt School has been distinguished by enduring beliefs in a well-rounded education, high performance standards, community involvement, and collaborative learning between the teacher and student. The purpose of this book is to embrace the past and look forward to our new chapters by exploring the genuine gift that The Hartt School has given to so many through the past century. As Malcolm Morrison expressed, students of the future are the "inheritors and representatives of a distinguished legacy." This portion of his 2006 commencement speech reflects the values of the founders and decades of visionary perspectives by Julius Hartt, Moshe Paranov, and the Hartt family, and provides a fitting close to this book.

" *It is not possible to plan everything and then copiously and unerringly follow that plan as we meet the future in the present. There are many influences well beyond our control. Life has a curious and exciting way of informing and directing us. We cannot perfectly and meticulously formulate a business plan for ourselves. We have also to be available to whatever adventure presents itself. Just as you rehearse a performance in order to explore the work and improve your facility to give the performance, you also have to be ready to respond to the particular circumstances of the evening and all that is attendant on this meeting of a moment with a particular audience and with a particular set of emotional and physical circumstances surrounding it. Therein lays the excitement: the performer and audience meet with the best intentions and expectations and then the true adventure starts.*

I encourage you to take that same leap with your lives. While holding to your ambitions and preparing yourselves for what the future MAY be: also allow yourselves to grow and respond to the immediacy of things. It may not be a perfectly predictable or even apparently relevant experience but your availability to the experiences may offer you surprises and certainly will contribute to your development as artists. Through your readiness to accept unexpected ideas you will most certainly learn. As Oliver Wendell Holmes said, "Man's mind, once stretched by a new idea, never regains its original dimension."

ACKNOWLEDGMENTS

I was fortunate to have a Centennial Committee of alums and faculty, many of whom have been part of Hartt's history for decades and were immensely helpful in compiling this pictorial history. To each of them, we owe a great deal of gratitude for their service to the school and guidance with this book and initiatives planned for the Hartt 100 celebration in years 2020–21.

HARTT CENTENNIAL COMMITTEE	
Linda Blotner	Dick Provost
Maggie Francis	Wayne Rivera
Steve Gryc	Debra Ryder
Patrick Miller	Peter Woodard
Johanna Morrison	

Numerous faculty and staff from every division and department of the school as well as friends and alums contributed historical memory and accuracy through their proofreading and interviews. The genuine support of University of Hartford president Gregory Woodward, Larry Alan Smith, dean of The Hartt School; Steve Metcalf; the Julius Hartt Board of Trustees (a special thanks to Jim Barry and Marcos Carreras); and the devoted faculty and staff of The Hartt School is truly a reflection of the spirit of our school from its founding.

We are most grateful for the support from the Hartford Foundation for Public Giving in helping make this publication possible, and to Suzanna Tamminen, director and editor-in-chief of Wesleyan University Press. Suzanna's patience and enthusiasm for this project made the work rewarding and gratifying.

The University of Hartford archivist, Sean Parke, contributed copious amounts of time, guidance, and expertise to the research process. Without his patient and knowledgeable support, this book and the celebration of Hartt's history could not have been accomplished in such depth and breadth. We are all indebted to him for his genuine and diligent efforts to preserve the history of The Hartt School and the University of Hartford. It is my hope that further research is conducted in the vast resources of the university archives. So much is yet to be unlocked.

John Reuter, photography instructor for the Hartford Art School, graciously involved his students in his PHO 340 class in preparing photographs of artifacts, which are found throughout the book.

Additionally, I am extremely grateful for my two student assistants, Alex Small, a double major in music management and violin, and Rachel Rosa, a 2019 graduate in visual communication design at the Hartford Art School.

Alex, who served as my production manager, enthusiastically sleuthed the photographers and sought permissions for the many images in the book, and compiled a list of faculty based on faculty pages of university catalogues since 1957, which will be made available on the Hartt 100 website in the spring of 2020. I am so grateful that Alex approached his work with the determination of a prime investigator. Without it we could not have used many of the wonderful images in the book or have honored the many faculty and staff that served our institution so devotedly.

I am extremely thankful for Rachel's extraordinary artistic perception in the layout and design of the book. She created grace and beauty that brought the colorful, historic Hartt characters to life. Support for her work was provided by the Women's Advancement Initiative from Dorothy Goodwin.* Rachel made this book a keepsake, a visual treasure, and a reflection of our very special school. John Nordyke, professor of visual communication design in the Hartford Art School, was tirelessly enthusiastic and helpful in his mentorship and guidance in this effort. John stepped in to finish the graphic design when Rachel graduated and became employed as a full-time designer. Thank you, Rachel, for creating a beautiful book in celebration of The Hartt School and John for seeing the project through to its completion.

For the past eighteen months I have interviewed scores of Hartt faculty, alums, and staff who have provided valuable memories and information. Many of the interviews were recorded and are preserved in the archives for future research.

And, finally, to my husband, Eric Hansen, who steadfastly supported and encouraged me throughout the past two years of intense research and writing, in addition to the challenges of university professorship. I look forward to our retirement and being able to make up precious time together!

Through photos and words I hoped to capture and celebrate the spirit of The Hartt School so that the tenacity and beliefs of its founders, and those that carried their torch, live on for another one hundred years. Many thanks to all involved for their enthusiasm, passion, and joyful memories that made this book possible.

UNIVERSITY OF HARTFORD

THE WOMEN'S ADVANCEMENT INITIATIVE
CONTINUING THE LEGACY OF HARTFORD COLLEGE FOR WOMEN

* The Women's Advancement Initiative at the University of Hartford is proud to continue the legacy of advancing each woman's potential in the Hartford College for Women tradition. This support does not necessarily imply endorsement by the University of Hartford or the Women's Advancement Initiative of research conclusions.

Appendix
The Hartt School Staff

The historical accounting of The Hartt School would not be complete without mention of the dedicated staff members who have been the pillars of its operations through time. Many administrators and staff members have been mentioned through the decades in the book; therefore this section serves as a thank you to those who have served in the recent past, listed chronologically.

Dean's Office: executive assistants
Nancy Lou Brown
Phillip Grover
Priscilla Mulvaney

Dean's Office: administration
Barbara Haksteen
David Bell
Clark Saunders
Robert Davis
Donna Menhart

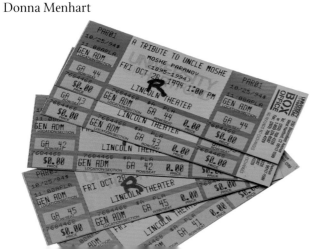

Admissions
Leila Hawken
Lynn Johnson
Erin Arrison
Laurie Marotta (Data Analyst)
Megan Abernathy
Rebecca Gould
Neal Humphreys
Claire Paik
Jan Rust

Public Relations
Lori Cartwright
Sherri Ziccardi
Chiara Leone (Gigline)
Ashley Fedigan

Hartt Operations:
scheduling, mailroom, and facilities
Jason Davis
Walter Gibson
John Holder and the C Team
Leonard Bretton
Dale Smith
Houston Smith

Student Services
Lynn Wronker
Barbara Johnson

Division Coordinators

In 1993 Dean Larry Alan Smith hired or reassigned staff members to serve as coordinators for the various divisions of the school. Several coordinators' titles were production managers prior to being titled coordinators.

Choral-Vocal
Barbara Porter

Jazz
Shauntice Marshall

Instrumental Studies
Ann Griffin
Karen Peters

Academic Studies
Natalie Wing

Music Education
Meghan Fouracre
Paula Trebra
Ann Brown

Theatre
Debbie Markowitz

Costumes
Marla Perlstein

Performing Arts Technology
Lief Ellis

Summerterm Kodály Choir and Clark Saunders teaching

REFERENCES

With exception of the references listed below, all photographs, artifacts, and quotes in this book are property of the University of Hartford, housed in the University Archives or in university electronic files. The University of Hartford provided permission to reprint this material.

Kassel, Matthew. "Javon Jackson Extends the Tradition," *DownBeat*, January 14, 2019, 19.

McCray, Kent. *The Man Behind the Most Beloved Television Shows*. Belen, New Mexico: Marianne Rittner-Holmes and Kent McCray, 18.

Primack, Bret. "Jackie McLean: Man with a Mission." *Jazz Educators Journal* 31, no. 1 (1998): 37.

Shanley, Mike. "For Prosperity's Sake: Music Schools Adopt Artist Legacy Programs." *Jazz Education Guide* (2008–2009): 38.

Schwager, Myrone. "A Contribution to the Biography of Ernest Bloch." *Current Musicology* 28 (1979): 42.

Watrous, Peter. "Jackie McLean Is Back with His Alto Sax after 20 Years Away." *New York Times*, April 25, 1990, 26.

INDEX

Page numbers in *italics* indicate illustrations.

Academic Studies Department, 62, 65
Adaskin Trio, 80
Adsit, Glen, *49*, 82
Aeolian Hall, 7
African American Music Department, 84
Alfred C. Fuller Music Center, 33
Allen, Larry D., 46
Allen Library. *See* Mildred P. Allen Memorial Library
Allen Memorial Fund, 58
Allen, Mildred P., 58
Alvarez, Manny, 89, 97
American Brass Quintet, 74
Amira, John, 77
Anderson, Marian, 33, 37
Apollo Theater, 83
Arms, Janet, 80
Army of the United States of America, Fort Devens, Massachusetts, 6
Aronson, Stanley, 80
Artist's Collective, The, 83, 84
Ashens, Robert, 99
Asylum Hill Congregational Church, 93
Avitsur, Haim, 74

Babel, Gregory, 76, 88
Bacon, Ethyl, 59, 92, 104
Baldwin, Ralph, 29, 42
Baltrucki, Matt, 105
Barefield, Robert, 96
Barney School of Business, 26
Barrueco, Manuel, 75
Barry, James, *86*, 112
Bauer, Harold, 8, *12*, 15, 16, *17*, 18, 22, 75
Benny, Jack, 33
Berkman Auditorium, 12, 108
Berkman, Daniel, 14
Berkman, John, *13*
Berkman, Samuel, 1, *12*, *13*, 15, *17*, 22, 31, *32*, *34*, 61, 75, 87
Berkshire Choral Festival, 52
Bernstein, Leonard, 37, 78,
Beth El Temple, 18
Beth Israel Synagogue, 29
Bishop, Addie, 93
Black, Robert, 78
Blakey, Art, 83
Bloch, Ernest, 3, 10, 15, 17, 64, 66
Blocker-Glynn, Noah, 53, 54
Blood, Curt, 80
Blotner, Linda Solow, 59, 112
Blue Note, 83, 85
Boccato, Rogerio, 77
Bolcom, William, 66
Bolkovac, Edward, 64, *94*, 95
Bombeck, Erma, 101
Bonacini, Renato, 78

Bond, Julian, 37
Borror, Ronald, 74
Boston's Jordan Hall, 7
Boston Symphony Orchestra (BSO), 7, 74,
Bowler, Phil, 84
Brahm's Requiem, 95
Brass Collegium, 64
Brass Ring Quintet, 47
Braus, Ira, 65
Brigadoon, 108
Broadhead, Edward H., 31, 59
Bronne, Ariana, 79
Bronstein, Raphael, 79
Brooker, Susan, 53
Brouwer, Leo, 75
Brown, Adrianne, 21
Brown, Esther Hinds, 44
Budries, David, 104, 105, 106
Bushnell Memorial Hall, 29, 33
Byard, Jaki, 84

Cage, John, 66
Caluda, Cherie, *96*
Camerata School of Music and Dance, 47
Campbell, Nola, 89
Campernaria, Miguel, 53
Capitol Symphonic Winds, 50
Carl, Robert, 63, 67, 68
Carlson, Michael, 64
Carmina Burana, 94
Carmen, 72
Carreras, Marcos, *86*, 112
Casey, Chris, 84
Castro, Luis de Mauro, 46, 75
Cathedral of Saint Joseph, 95
Cecelia Club of Hartford, 7, 12
Chapdelaine, Jim, 105
Cheney Hall, 107
Cheney, Tim, 62, 68
Children's Musical Theater, 11
Children's Singing School, 11, 44
Choral Club of Hartford, 7
Choral Collegium, 64
Christensen, Robert, 44, 94
Chung, Yousun, 80
Clark, Edward, 74, 76
Clemente, Peter, *75*
Cleveland Institute, 17
Cobb, Kevin, 74
Coffee, Rick, 94
Coffin, Vincent (and Mrs.), *30*
Cohen, Irene, (See Irene Kahn), 13
College Band Director's National Assoc., 81
Colon, Javier, 96
Composition Department, 66, 97
Concert Ensemble, 69
Concert Orchestra, 48
Concerto for Mallet Instruments, 77
Conley, Irene, 106
Connecticut Commission on the Arts, 84

Connecticut Advisory Committee on Music Education, 12
Connecticut Center for Early Childhood in Music and Movement, 47
Connecticut Children's Chorus, 48, 52
Connecticut Historical Society, Hartford, 14
Connecticut Opera Association, 99
Connecticut State Board of Education, 29, 31, 43, 87
Connecticut Youth Symphony, 48, 49
Contemporary Music Festival, 81
Contemporary Studies Department/Division, 104
Cook, Karen, 65
Coolidge Quartet, 23
Cooper, Betsy, 105
Copland, Aaron, 28, 36, *37*, 66, 93
Corbell, Claude, 96
Corigliano, John, 66
Cowell, Henry, 28
Creative Studies Program, 55
Cremisis, Julius, 45
Cumming, Edward, 80, 81, *96*
Curtis School, 51

D'Addio, Daniel, *48*, 49, 50
Daetsch, Melinda, 79
Dance Connecticut, 60, 71
David, Barbara, 79
Davis, Annmarie, 109
Davis, Miles, 83
Davis, Robert, 109
Davis, Steve, 84, 85
Dean, Allan, 73
Dede, Mehmet, 107
DeLibero, Phil, 80
Dempsey, John (Governor), 58
Diard, William, 93
Diemente, Edward, 29, 36, *66, 67*, 104
Dinerstein, Norman, 68
Don Giovanni, 91
Dorothy Goodwin Women's Advancement Initiative, 112
Doty, Al, 21
DownBeat Hall of Fame, 85
Drake, Emmett, 50
Duffy, Ward, 30
Dunster, Samantha, 53
Dvorak, Wayne, 88

Eastman School of Music, 42, 51
Eckhart, Janet, 88
Educational Lyric Theatre, 108
Einfeld, David, 47, 49, *50*
Einfeld, Teri, 47, 49, *50*
Einstein, Alfred, 10, 23, 63
Ellington, Duke, 82
Ellington Dances, 72
Ellis, Lief, 72
Emerson String Quartet, 79, 80, 106

Engle, Susan, 88
Epstein, Alvin, 67
Ernest Block Society, 18

Farkas, Alexander, 88, 94
Farmington High School, 19
Farmington Schools, 8
Feierabend, John, 47, 48, 52, 89, *90*, 94
Feierabend, Lillie, 89, *90*
Feldman, Morton, 66
Feldman, Rabbi A. J., *29*, 30
Felstein, Robert, 109
Fernwood School, 10
Ferrebee, Sallie, 52
Fiertek, Michelle, 96
Finkle, David, 106
First Catalogue, The, (1920–1921), 14, *15*, 17
Flagg, Aaron, 54, 72, 103
Flater, Tracy, 52
Foot in the Door Ensemble, 69, 81, 82
Ford Foundation, The, 108
Forte, Allen, 65
Franchetti, Arnold, 34, 36, 38. 66, 67, 75
Francis, Alan, *54*, 55, 80
Francis, Margreet (Maggie), *54*, 76, 112
Freed, Isadore, 66
Freedman, Stanley, 82
Friese-Lepak Timpani Method, 77
Fuller, Alfred C., 27, *28*, 30, 76
Fuller at 50, 103,
Fuller Brush Company, 27
Fuller, Mary Primrose, *33*, 36
Fuller (Music) Building, 13, 44, 105, 108
Fund for Access, 51, 52

Gabrilowitch, Ossip, 8
Galeota, Joe, 77
Garbousova, Raya, 78
Gautier, Eva, 15
Gekker, Chris, 74
Gengras Student Union, 26, 37, 108
George, Mark, 53, 54
Ghilia, Oscar, 75
Ghittalia, Armando, 74
Gibson, Walter, 61
Gillespie, Dizzy, 84
Glastonbury Schools, 8, 51
Glazier, Joan, 44
Glen Miller Band, 80
Goldberg, Marc, 80
Goldfarb, Robert and Frankie, 103
Goldmark, Rubin, 10
Goldovsky, Boris, 92
Goodrich, Kathleen, 89
Goodwin, Francis, 8
Gottschalk, Nathan, 31, 34, 43
Grasso, Ella, 84
Gray, Kevin, 109
Greater Hartford Community Chorus, 42, 44, 94

Greater Hartford Youth Chorale, 94
Greater Hartford Youth Orchestra (GHYO), 45, 49,
Greater Hartford Youth Wind Ensemble, 48, 49
Greenblatt, Harmon, 106
Green, Ryan Speedo, 96
Greenwood, Connie, 55
Gress-Miles Organ, *76*
Gryc, Steve, *66*, 67, 112

Hagen, Julie, 89
Hall High School, 36
Hamilton, 96
Handel, Mort and Irma Performing Arts Center (HPAC), 52, 108
Hanks, Thompson, 73
Hansel and Gretel, Humperdinck, 45, 91
Hansen, Dee, 89
Hanson, Raymond, 36, 75
Harmony Winds, 55
Harris, Donald, *45*, 46, 47, 62, 68, 84, 97
Harrison Libraries, 59
Harrison, Walter, 73, 101, 103
Harry Jack Gray Center, 59, 61
Hartford Art School, 19, 30, 31, 34, 97, 112
Hartford Ballet, (School), 52, 60, 70, 71
Hartford Chorale, 52, 95
Hartford College of Women, 60, 108
Hartford Conservatory, 47
Hartford Foundation for Public Giving, 52, 112
Hartford High School, 12, 57
Hartford Hospital Chorus, 8
Hartford Hospital Training School Glee Club, 7
Hartford Monthly, 19
Hartford Musical Foundation, Inc., 20
Hartford Oratorio Society, the, 7
Hartford School of Music, 20
Hartford Seminary, 20
Hartford Symphony Society, 36
Hartford Symphony Orchestra, 8, 20, 29, 45, 52, 67, 73, 74, 76, 80, 81, 95, 99, 101
Hartford Theological Seminary (Hartford Seminary Foundation), 29
Hartford Times, 3, 10
Hartford Universalist Church, 50
Hartford Youth Chorale, 94
Hartford Youth Orchestra, 43
Hartt Big Band, 84
Hartt Board of Trustees (Directors), 16, 22, 28, 29, 100, 112
Hartt Centennial Committee, 112
Hartt Chamber Choir, 95
Hartt Chamber Orchestra, 64
Hartt Chorale and Chorus, 34, 95
Hartt College of Music, 26, 27, 29, 30, 31, 32, 33, 34, 42, 57, 64, 71, 73. 78, 80, 87, 88, 92, 96, 97

Hartt College of Music Opera Department, 91, 107
Hartt College of Music Symphony Orchestra, 33, 36, 37
Hartt Collegium, 74
Hartt Commencement Orchestra, 100
Hartt Community Division (HCD), 45, 47, 48, 53, 53, 54, 71
Hartt Concerto Competition 64
Hartt, Harriet (Gizzy), 3
Hartt Instrument and Performance Library, 61
Hartt, Jennie (Jane), 3
Hartt, Julius, *2, 6*, 10, 12, 15, 16, 17, 20, 53, 64, 91, 111
Hartt Library, 58
Hartt Hall of Fame, 63
Hartt Opera Department, 70, 93
Hartt Opera (Music) Theater, 10, 14, 93, 108
Hartt Opera Theater Guild, 36, 92
Hartt, Pauline (Dot), (Paranov), 1, 7, *10, 11*, 15, 19, 31, 91
Hartt Preparatory Academy, 53
Hartt, Robert, 3, 2
Hartt School of Music. *See* Julius Hartt School of Music
Hartt School, The, 53, 71, 100, 101, 103, 105, 107, 108, 109, 111, 112
Hartt School Dance Division, 71
Hartt Steelband, 77
Hartt String Quartet, 79
Hartt Suzuki Institute, 49, 50
Hartt Symphonic Wind Ensemble, 36, 38, 74, 81,
Hartt Symphony Orchestra, 81
Harvey, Peter, 46
Haston, Warren, 89
Hayes, Peggy Lyman, 71
Heck, George, 8
Hepburn, Katharine, 19
Herman, Gabe, 105, 106
Hess, Myra, 29
Higdon, Jennifer, 66
Hill, Barbara, 74
Hill, James, 80
Hillyer College, 8, 19, 30, 31, 108
Hindemith, Paul, 91
Hinds, Esther, 93
Hintz, Elmer, 87
Hirschfeld Al, 99
Holcomb, Al, 89
Holm, Hanya, 69
Holtz, John, 76
Horace Bushnell Memorial Hall, 7
Horsted, Kelly, 96
Hubbard, Helen, 34
Huffman, Kristin, 109
Hugh, Robert, 52

Iadone, Joseph, 74
Infinity Hall, 107
Ingraham, Paul, 73
Institute of Musical Art of the Juilliard Foundation, 18
Institute of Contemporary American Music (ICAM), 28, 66, 97
Instrumental Studies Department (Division), 76
In the Service of the Beautiful, 24
Invasion of Cambodia, 37

Jackie McLean Institute of Jazz, 65, 84, 86
Jackson, Douglas, 89
Jackson, James III, 74
Jackson, Javon, 86
Jacobi, Frederick, 66
Jazz and Popular Music Institute, 55
Jazz Department (JMI), 82, 103
Jazz Messengers, 83
Jacob's School of Music, 51
Jerigan, Kemp, 80
Johannesen, Grant, 36, 99
John, Erik (Horace Everett), 93, *94*
Johnny Appleseed, (Carmino Ravosa)45
Johnson, Gilbert, 74
Jordon, James, 89
Julius Hartt Board of Trustees, 30, 38, 61, 63, 112
Julius Hartt College of Music, 20, *21*, 43, 69, 74, 84, 91
Julius Hartt, Moshe Paranov and Associated Teachers, 12
Julius Hartt Musical Foundation (JHMF), 5, 20, 24, 27, 28, 36, 62, 66, 91
Julius Hartt School of Music, The, *viii*, 10, *14*, 16, 17, 18, 20, 23, 25, 28, 29, 32, 33, 33, 36, 42, 43, 45, 58, 62, 66, 69, 83, 87, 92, 97, 100
Julius Hartt School of Music Scholarship Fund, 44
Julius Hartt School of Music Training Orchestra, *43*
Juilliard School, 50, 60, 72

Kahn, Irene, (Berkman), *13, 14*, 15, 19, *34*, 61, 75, 91
Kaltakchian, Sarkis, 53
Karas, Joza, 64
Karr, Gary, *78*
Kaschmann, Truda, 69, *70*
Keller, Anthony, 84
Kelly, Sondra, 96
Kennedy Center Awards, 64, 70
Khachaturian, Aram, 68
King, Terry, 79
Kingswood (Oxford) School, 10, 12, 51
Kiwanis Club, 12
Kleeman, Rose, *34*
Klingenberg, Krystal, 65
Klock, Lynn, 81

Kodály Method, 65, 89
Kramer, David, 55
Koffman, Carrie, 80
Koscielny, Anne, 36, 75
Kosloff, Doris, 94
Koussevitsky, Serge (Mrs. Olga), *37*, 78
Kurtz, Justin, 105

Ladd, Christopher, *75*
Landsdale, Katie, 79
Lane, Mrs. George, 58
Langton, Stephen, 30, 31, 34
Larson, Steve, 79
Lawrence, Robert, 93
Leary, Timothy, 37
Lee, John, 30
Lepak, Alexander, 46, *77*, 84
Letters of a Musician, 1917–1918, 2, *3*, 15
Letter to a Young Man, 1918, 3
Levine, Arthur, 46
Levy, Johanna, 96
Lewin, David, 65
Lichtmann, Jay, 74
Life and Adventures of Nickolas Nickelby, 109
Lifton, Deborah, 96
Lila Acheson Wallace Library of The Juilliard School, 60
Lilly, Pauline, 10
Lion's Gate Trio, 80
Lischner, Rose, *87*
Little Sweep, The (Benjamin Britten), 45
Lodge, John, 58
Logan, Cameron, 65
Lopatnikoff, Nikolai, 66
Los Angeles Guitar Quartet, 75
Los Angeles Philharmonic, 51
Lucarelli, Bert, 46
Luening, Otto, 66
Lurie, Bernard, *45*
Lynn, Enid, 53, *69*, 71
Lyons, Gilda, 68

Macbride, David, *68*
MacDowell Award, 82
Mace, Ray, 74
Mack, Gerald, 45, 94
Madsen, Carl, 55
Malcolm X, 37
Manfredi, Amy Lesko, 71
Manufacturers Association of Connecticut, 27
Marble, Tracey, 109
Markowitz, Debbie, 109
Martha Graham Dance Company, 71
Mark Twain House, 8
Marx, Josef, 78
Marijosius, Vytautas, 36, 43, 68, *81*
Marriage of Figaro, 91
Mattran, Donald, 36, 80, 88, 97
McCray, Kent, 107
McGill University, 105

McIlroy, William, 34
McLean, Dollie, 84, *86*
McLean, Jackie, 38, 46, 82, *83*, 84, *96*, 105
McLean, Melonaé, 84, *86*
McLean, René, *83*, 85
McLean, Vernone, 84
McLellan, Dave, *75*
Menapace, Michael, 81
Mendelssohn, Felix, *Elijah*, 44
Mende, Rose, 76, 80, 87
Mendoker, Scott, 74
Menhart, Donna, 65
Menuhin, Yehudi, 64
Metcalfe, Scott, 105
Metcalf, Steve, 80, 101, 103, 112
Metropolitan Opera, 23, 96, 99
Miami String Quartet, 80
Middletown Public Schools, 51
Mildred P. Allen Memorial Library, 58, 59, 61
Millard Auditorium, 103, 108
Miller, Anton, 79
Miller, Edward, 67
Miller, Gary, 93
Miller, Patrick, *62*, 63, 112
Miller-Porfiris Trio, 80
Mingus, Charles, 83
Minneapolis Orchestra, 51
Miranda, Lin-Manuel, 96
Moller-Marino, Diana, 109
Monk, Thelonious, 83
Monteiro, Shawnn, 86
Moore, Kermit, 79
Moore, Tracey, 109
Morales, Hilda, 72
Mori, Akane, 65
Morrison, Johanna, *102*, 109, 112
Morrison, Malcolm, 54, 95, 99, 100, 101, *102*, 103, 108, 111, 112
Morrison, Watson, 75
Mort and Irma Handel Performing Arts Center, *102*
Mortensen Library, 59
Moses, Fritz, 96
Mount Holyoke College, 18
Mount Saint Joseph Academy, 42
Much Ado About Nothing, 108
Mulready, Joseph, 45, *63*, 68, 100
Murtha, Janis, 73
Murtha, Roger, *73*, 74
Music Education Department (Division), 47, 87, 88
Music Industry Department, 104, 105, 106, 107
Music Library Association, 59
Music Management (MUM), 104,
Music Production and Technology (MPT), 69, 104, 105, 106
Music Teachers National Association (MTNA), 29
Music in Terezín, 64

Nagel, Robert, 73,
Nagy, Elemer, 10, 43, 91, 92, 107
National Association of College Wind and Percussion, 88
National Association of Schools of Music (NASM), 12, 47, 48, 87
National Endowment for the Arts, 67,
National Endowment for the Arts Jazz Master Award, 85
National Medal of the Arts, 70
NCATE, 87
Nelson, Koby, 105
Nelsova, Zara, 36
Neumann, Meredith, 52
New England Conservatory, 42, 97
New Haven Chorale, 95
New Horizons Band, 4
New Music Resources Grant, 67
New York Brass Quintet, 73
New York Metropolitan Opera Studio, 44
New York Philharmonic Young People's Concerts, 78
Ngai, Emlyn, 65, 74, 79
Nicholais, Alwin, 43, 69, *70*
Nordyke, John, 113
Nott, Kenneth, 62, *63*, 64, 74
Nutcracker, The, 71

Oakley, Paul, 94, 95
Oak National Chorus, 95
O'Flynn, Maureen, 96
Oliveira, Elmar, 79
Once on This Island, 108
Opera Workshop, 96
Orpheus in the Underworld, 95
Osborne, George, 99
Oshima, Ayako, 80
Opus '89 String Orchestra, 50

Palisca, Claude, 65
Paranov, Elizabeth (Libby) Warner, 15, *18, 19*, 31, 34, 36, 46
Paranov, Moshe, 1, 6, 7, 8, 9, 11, 12, *14*, 16, *17*, 18, 19, *22*, 23, 25, 27, 28, *30*, 31, *32, 34*, 36, 46, 53, 57, 61, 63, 68, 70, 71, 73, 75, 80, 81, 82, 84, 87, 91, *97*, 99, *100*, 103, 104
Paranov Fagan, Nina, *11*, 21, 33, *104*, 105, 111
Paranov, Pauline (see Pauline Hartt), 31, 91
Paranov, Tanya, *11*, 45
Parke, Sean, 112
Parker, Charlie, 83
Partridge, Gary, 50
Paulus, Carolyn, 109
Peabody, 105
Pellettieri, Gladys, 58
Pellettieri, Louis, 31, *34*, 42, 44, 53, 58
Percussive Arts Society Hall of Fame, 77
Performance 20/20, 69
Performing Arts Management, 104
Performer's Certificate Program, 48, 53

Performing Arts Management (PAM), 106
Perkins, Ralph, 72, 108, 109
Perlmutter, Morris, 1, 15, 17,
Perry, Pam, 94
Petruschka, 72
Philadelphia Orchestra, 74
Philharmonia Winds, 55
Pierce, Paul, 55
Pier, Stephen, 72,
Pike, John, 109
Piltzecker, Ted, 77
Piston, Walter, 66
Planner, Mark, 109
Playbill Magazine, 109
Porfiris, Rita, 79
Portland String Quartet, 99
Powell, Bud, 83
Pratt, Waldo Selden, 29
Prism Project, 55
Prodigal Son, 66
Provost, Richard, 46, *75*, 112
Pruitt, Jerry, 96
Public Works Concert Series, 66
Putsché, Thomas, 36, 67

Quarter Century Club, 92

Radnofsky, Ken, 81
Raiken, Larry, 109
Rao, Doreen, 52
Ralph Waldo Emerson, 7
Rascher, Sigurd, 80
Rauche, Benjamin, 65, 96
Rauche, Tony, 62
Real Artways, 107
Reese, Kim, 89
Reeves, Nat, *85*, 86
Reilly, Charles Nelson, 93
Renbrook School, 51
Respass, Hilary, 53, 54
Reuter, John, 112
Reynolds, Geoffrey, 89
Ribicoff, Governor, 31
Richard P. Garmany Chamber Music Series, 103
Richard P. Garmany Fund, 103
Richard P. Garmany Series, 80
Ridolfi, Robert, 79
Rivera, Wayne, 93, *94*, 96, 112
Robb, Madelyn, 19, 31
Robinson, Jenelle, 109
Rockefeller Foundation, 67
Roderick, 53
Rogers, Willard B., 8
Rojak, John, 74
Rollins, Sonny, 83
Rosa, Rachel, 112, 113
Rose, Leonard, 33, *34*, 36
Rostropovic, Mstislav, 7
Rubin, Jerry, 37

Rudnick, Tracey, 59
Rusack, Richard, 89
Russell, Joshua, 89
Russo, Matthew, 74
Rust, Alan, 108, 109
Ryder, Debra Collins, 72, 112

Sacred Service, The, 18
Satellites (Community Division), 46
Saunders, Clark, *89, 115*
Schar, Stuart, 97
Sellars, James, 62, 82
Shanahan, Shane, 77
Shearer, Greig, 80
Schenker, Heinrich, 62
Schiano, Michael, *63*, 65
School of Dance Connecticut, 52, 71
School of Music, North Carolina School of the Arts, 100
Schorr, Friedrich, 23
Schorr, Virginia, 34
Schuman, William, 66
Schuttenhelm, Thomas, 65
Schwager, Myron, 3, 62, 64
Schwerdtfeger, Wanda, 59
Segal, Rubin, 43
Sessions, Roger, 28
Shostakovich, Dimitri, 7
Silverherz, Dorothy, 70
Simsbury Schools, 8
Simsmore Square Satellite, 51
Sinfonia and Stringendo, 55
Sinta, Donald, 80, 81
Slugs Saloon, 83, 84
Small, Alex, 112, 113
Smith, Barbara, 88
Smith, Jackie, 55
Smith, Larry Alan, 52, 68, 71, *96, 100*, 101, 102, 108, 112
Smith, Neal, 50
Snedecor, Phil, 74
Sollenberger, Elizabeth, 76
Soni Fidelis Woodwind Quintet, 47
South Windsor School, 51
Sprout, Howard, *44*
Stamford Symphony, 103
Steen Ken, *67*, 103
St. Joseph College, 12, 14
St. Joseph's Cathedral. *See* Cathedral of Saint Joseph
Stern, Isaac, 33, *34*, 36, 108
Stevinson-Nollet, Katie, 72
Stoltz, Phyllis, 44
Street Scene, 94
Sugar Hill neighborhood, New York, 82
Suzuki Violin Method (Program-Orchestra), 44, 47, 48, 49, 50, 54, 55
Swallow, John, 73
Swann, Kyle, 96

Sylphide, 72
Swanson, Kathryn, 65
Symphony Society of Greater Hartford, 12
Synder, Kerala, 62

Tamminen, Suzanna, 112
Teal, Larry, 81
Telefunke, 107
Ten Maidens and No Man, 91
Tender Land, The, 93
Terry, Sue, 84
Tetel, Mihai, 79
Theatre Department/Division, 107
Thomas, Marcus, 107
Tompkins, Alan, 32
Thompson, Arthur, 44, 93, 99
Thomson, Virgil, 66
Thomas, Susan Knapp, 75
Thorton School of Music, 51
Tonkin, Humphrey, 79
Torrington Schools, 8
Toth, Benjamin, *77*
Tower, Joan 66,
Trachtenberg, Stephen Joel, 96, 97
Traggor, Philip, 34
Trinity Church, 64
Trinity Club, 12
Trinity College, 12
Trudel, Eric, 96
Tourel, Jennie, 93
Trial by Jury, 95
Turetzky, Bertram, 78
Turner, Charles, 65
Twain, Mark, 8,

University of Connecticut, 14
University of Hartford, 12, 19, 21, 26, 27, 37, 52, 53, 67, 96, 101, 112
University of Hartford Magnet School, 89
University of St. Joseph, 107
Urban, Bela, 104
US Coast Guard Band, 74
Uthoff, Michael, 99,

Verdi's *Requiem*, 95
Vieaux, Jason, 75
Viragh, Gabor, 65
Viragh, Katalin, 65
Virtuosi, 55
Vocal Studies, 91
Von Suppé, Franz, 91
Vytautas Marijosius Memorial Award in Orchestral Programming, 81

Wadsworth Atheneum, 12
Wakefield, David, 74
Walcott, Frederic, C., 12
Walcott, Martha Blake
Wallace, Lenzy, 46, 53
War in Vietnam, 37

Warwick, Dionne, *96*
Watkinson School, 8
Watson, David, 108, 109
Watt, Nina, 72
Weigl, Karl, 23
Weill, Kurt, 94
Weisfeld, Joni, 109
Wells, George Ross, 63,
Westfall, David, 76
Wesleyan University, 95
Wesleyan University Press, 112
Wethersfield Women's Chorus, 42
Whitaker, Greg, 74
Who Are the Blind (Mary Lynn Trombly), 45
Wilde Auditorium, 59
Willett, Bill, 88
Willheim, Imanuel, 38, 62, *63*, 64
Willis, Larry, *85*
Wilson, Alan, 30, 32
Winograd, Arthur, 67
Wion, John, 80
Woodard, Peter, 38, *81*, 85, 86, 112
Woodruff, Archibald M., 34, 92
Woodward, Gregory, 112
Worcester Choral Society, 94
Womack, Mark, 109
WRGB, Schenectady, New York, 91
WTIC Radio, 7

Yaffe, Michael, *46*, 47, 51, 52, 53, 54, 71, 108
Yakemore, Andrew, 51
Yakemore Family Performing Arts Center, 51
Yale Music Association Operas, 91
Yale Theatre School, Sound Design Department, 105
Yi, Chen, 66
Young, Lester, 83
Young People's Orchestra, 48
Younse, Stuart, 52, 89
Yueh, Chai-Lun, 96

Zavada-Machose, Kathleen, 105
Zei, Jack, 93
Zei, Joyce, 93
Zimmerman, Christopher, 81
Zukerman, Eugenia, 36
Zukerman, Pinchas, 36